Mountain Biking the Coast Range
Guide 4

Ventura County & the Sespe

WWW.THRIFTYOWL.COM

by Mickey McTigue

Edited by Sue Irwin

Photographs by Mickey McTigue, Linda McTigue,
Richard Mason and Doug Adler

Original maps by Mickey McTigue
with computer adaptation by Sue Irwin

FINE EDGE
Productions
BISHOP, CALIFORNIA

ACKNOWLEDGMENTS

The author wishes to thank the many people whose help and knowledge made this publication possible, including my wife, Linda; my children, Corey, Marcie, Murray and Amanda; and my publishers, Don and Réanne Douglass.

Special thanks to: Richard Mason, who explored with me from the early years; Hank Maynard, for transportation to new places; Louis Andaloro, condor biologist; Don Lenzi; Gary Vose; Ray Reed; Bill Dorsey; David Haney and John Boggs, Ojai Ranger District; Beth Wallace-Terry, Point Mugu State Park Ranger; Lon Haldeman, ultra-marathon cyclist; and Jim Young, gold miner.

Important Disclaimer

Mountain biking is a potentially dangerous sport in which serious injury and death can and do occur. Trails have numerous natural and man-made hazards, and conditions may change constantly. Most of the routes in this book are not signed or patrolled. This book may contain errors and omissions and is not a substitute for proper instruction, experience and preparedness.

You must accept full and complete responsibility for yourself while bicycling. The authors, editors, publishers, land manager, distributors, retailers and others associated with this book are not responsible for errors or omissions and do not accept liability for any loss or damage incurred from using this book.

CONTENTS

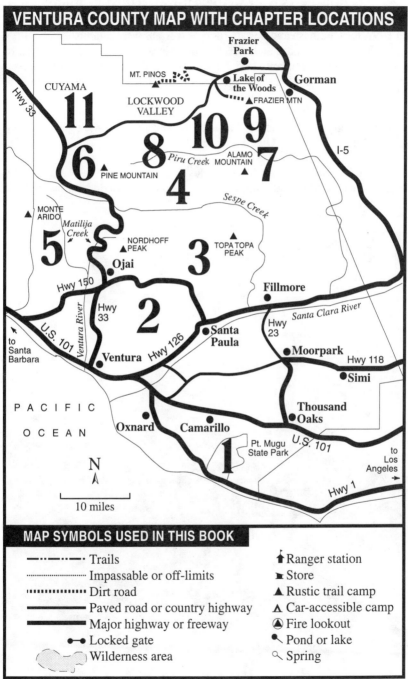

VENTURA COUNTY MAP WITH CHAPTER LOCATIONS

Frazier
Park

Hwy 33

CUYAMA

MT. PINOS

LOCKWOOD
VALLEY

11

6

PINE MOUNTAIN

Lake of
the Woods

Gorman

FRAZIER MTN

10 **9**

8 Piru Creek

ALAMO
MOUNTAIN

7

I-5

4

Sespe Creek

MONTE
ARIDO

Matilija
Creek

NORDHOFF
PEAK

5

TOPA TOPA
PEAK

3

Ojai

Fillmore

Hwy 150

Hwy
33

2

Santa Clara River

Hwy
23

Hwy 126

Santa
Paula

Moorpark

U.S. 101

Ventura River

Ventura

Hwy 118

to
Santa
Barbara

Simi

PACIFIC

OCEAN

Thousand
Oaks

Oxnard

Camarillo

1

Pt. Mugu
State Park

U.S. 101

to
Los
Angeles

N

Hwy 1

10 miles

MAP SYMBOLS USED IN THIS BOOK

— ·· — ·· — · Trails

Impassable or off-limits

Dirt road

Paved road or country highway

Major highway or freeway

Locked gate

Wilderness area

Ranger station

Store

Rustic trail camp

Car-accessible camp

Fire lookout

Pond or lake

Spring

Publisher's Note to the All-New Third Edition

In 1992, the Chumash and Sespe Wilderness Areas were established, resulting in the loss of many roads and trails to mountain bicycling. This all-new Third Edition brings you Mickey McTigue's latest research on a number of alternate trails that offset those losses. Mickey's work has helped turn a potential mountain biking vacuum into a wealth of backcountry routes.

For information on Wilderness boundaries and regulations, please call the USFS Ranger Station in Ojai, 805-646-4348.

By carefully following the IMBA Rules of the Trail (see page 95) and by assisting with trail maintenance and supervision, you can do your part to keep trails open to cycling.

INTRODUCTION

I learned to ride a bicycle on a farm in Vermont where most of the rural roads were graded dirt. My family moved to Ojai, California, in 1954 and the dirt fire roads in the nearby National Forest were similar, so riding a bicycle there seemed like a natural thing to do. Riding-single track trails was the next logical step. From 1957 until 1960, about six of us friends rode often and explored many miles of roads and trails. It was during this time we made many overnight camping trips and every winter went down the Sespe and stayed at the Hot Springs for three or four days. Travel, wars, marriage, careers, and children left us with less riding time, but I still made occasional trips over the next 20 years.

In the early 1980s, better-equipped bicycles became available, and more people entered the sport of mountain bicycling. Local newspaper articles occasionally described the riding adventures of people in the area, and I contacted some of them, including Don and Réanne Douglass. We started riding together on a regular basis, and I did a lot of the planning because of my extensive local knowledge. Don kept on persuading me to write a guidebook, but I didn't believe many people would be interested in a sport that took so much hard physical effort. I finally relented because I saw more and more people out riding, some with no idea of where they were going and with a lot of wrong information that had been passed off to them as fact.

After a year of exploring and logging information, and late nights writing and rewriting, the first edition of Guide 4 came out. I still didn't believe it would be popular — was I ever surprised. I had been riding for 20 years, never seeing another rider I didn't know (and not many of them either), but suddenly this obscure sport I was into exploded. Now bicycle tracks are all over, and on most trips you'll see more cyclists than hikers and horse riders combined. The better roads and trails have a smooth, wheel-carved track.

In our area, lack of a consistent long-term forest plan resulted in management practices that wasted funds and damaged resource capabilities. A series of acts were passed to correct this situation, starting with the Multiple Use Act of 1960 and continuing on through the National Forest Management Act of 1976, which requires a specific Forest Plan. Meetings were held for public input, and finally in 1988 the revised Forest Plan was adopted.

The Forest Plan required the management of large areas of roadless land in order to preserve wilderness values. On June 16, 1992, a wilderness bill was signed into law creating 287,450 acres of wilderness, primarily in Ventura County. Since the Wilderness Act of 1964 prohibited the use of mechanized vehicles in wilderness areas (instead of motor vehicles as originally proposed), bicycles were automatically prohibited in the new local wilderness areas.

Most of the debate on the local wilderness bills during the last four years centered on water issues. There was almost no mention of bicycles, so when it became law most people weren't aware that bicycles were prohibited. We may not like it but this situation won't change for a long time. That's the law and we have to live with it. Losing the Sespe and the Hot Springs is the worst, since they have no equal. The other trails now off limits are mostly remote, rough trails that were seldom used, and then only by advanced riders. Future maintenance will be at primitive trail standards, making them unsuitable for bicycles anyway. Fortunately, there are still a great many riding trails outside the wilderness areas, and of course, there are many fun fire roads.

Ironically, almost 50 miles of non-wilderness roads and trails have been abandoned. This is due to lack of use or by private property blocking public access. Sometimes trails that are not popular with hikers or equestrians due to distance or lack of water are fine for bicyclists. Others are not shown on recent maps or have changed and are hard to find. When access is blocked by private property, it's usually near the beginning of the road or trail, so the entire route becomes unavailable to the public. Scarce maintenance funds are spent on trails that receive the most use, while seldom-used trails deteriorate quickly and soon fade away.

The Forest Plan emphasizes improved access by negotiating with landowners to gain easements through gifts, trades, purchases, or condemnation. But with funding at 70% or less, easement monies are hard to come by. Where demand is high, connecting trails are built around private land, abandoned roads and trails are reopened, and maintenance levels are increased.

The Forest Service is capable of helping us get the type of roads and trails we want. In most cases they are willing but don't have the money. The first step toward helping them help you is to let them know where you ride and what your needs are. Send them a card or letter, or give them a call. They want to know. The next step is even better — volunteer for a trail crew. They can get excited about that! The Forest Service will provide tools, transportation, training, and insurance. You provide the labor, but work at your own pace. I have done this many times during the last four years, and I am amazed at how satisfying it is. I would rather cut brush in the forest all day than trim my hedge at home. The Forest Service personnel here are dedicated, hard-working people who can do a lot if you help them. Be a part of the solution — give them a call at (805) 646-4348.

MOUNTAIN BIKE TOURING IN LOS PADRES NATIONAL FOREST
Special Considerations

Guide 4 covers Ventura County, California, from sea level at the beach to nearly 9,000 feet at the summit of Mt. Pinos, with wide ranges in climate, elevation, trail and road conditions, and areas of remoteness. Good preparation will provide opportunities for pleasure. Poor preparation can bring disaster. We offer the following suggestions as a minimum guide for exploring Ventura County backcountry by mountain bike. The guidebook was written to help others enjoy bike touring on the forest roads and trails as I have for the last 30 years. Mountain bike touring has been a way to extend my range and see places I wouldn't get to see otherwise.

Courtesy: Know and follow the IMBA Rules of the Trail printed in the Appendix. Extend courtesy to all other trail users and follow the golden rule. The trails and roads in Ventura County are used by hikers, equestrians, fishermen, hunters and oil/mine operators, who all feel proprietary about the use of the trails. Mountain bikes are newcomers here.

Preparations: Plan your trip carefully by developing a check list. Know your abilities and your equipment. Prepare to be self-sufficient at all times.

Mountain Conditions: Be prepared for:
- Sun: Protect your skin against the sun's harmful rays. The higher you go, the more damaging the sun can become. Use sunscreen with a rating of 15 or more. Wear light colored long-sleeved shirts or jerseys, and a hat with a wide brim. Guard against heatstroke in these desert-like mountains by riding in early morning or late afternoon when the sun's rays are less intense.
- Low Humidity: Start each trip with at least 4 full water bottles or more. *Gallons* of water may not be sufficient for *really* hot weather. Force yourself to drink, whether or not you feel thirsty. Untreated drinking water may cause Giardiasis or other diseases. Carry water from a known source, or treat it.
- Variations in Temperature: You may find it cool and foggy on the coastal side of a ridge, and hot and dry on the other. Carry extra clothing—a windbreaker, gloves, stocking cap—and use the multi-layer system so you can adjust according to conditions. Keep an eye on changing cloud and wind conditions.
- Wind: Wind, as well as changes in weather, can deplete your energy. Sluggish or cramping muscles and fatigue indicate the need for calories. Carry high-energy snack foods such as granola bars, dried fruits and nuts to maintain strength and warmth, and add clothing layers as the temperature drops or the wind increases.
- Winter storms in these mountains can be dangerous, with thunderstorms, swollen creeks, and major dumps of snow at higher elevations. Avoid storms by checking forecasts and changing your plans to fit the weather. Don't

attempt trips requiring major stream crossings during threatening weather.
   • Know how to deal with dehydration, hypothermia, altitude sickness, sunburn or heatstroke. Be sensitive at all times to the natural environment; the land can be frightening and unforgiving. If you break down, it may take you longer to walk out than it took you to ride in! Check with your local Red Cross, Sierra Club, or mountaineering textbooks for detailed information.

Respect the Environment: Minimize your impact on the natural environment. *Remember, mountain bikes are not allowed in Wilderness Areas and in certain other restricted areas.* Ask, when in doubt; you are a visitor. Leave plants and animals alone; historic and cultural sites untouched. Stay on established roads and trails, and do not enter private property. Follow posted instructions and use good common sense. Don't be a "Backcountry Pioneer" who strays from established trails, spoiling untouched terrain, and ruining the name of mountain biking for the rest of us.

Control and Safety: Control your mountain bike at all times. Guard against excessive speed. Avoid overheated rims and brakes on long or steep downhill rides. Lower your center of gravity by lowering your seat on downhills. Lower your tire pressure on rough or sandy stretches. Avoid hunting season. (Ask local sporting goods stores which areas are open to hunting.) Use appropriate safety equipment, such as helmet, gloves, protective clothing, etc. Carry first aid supplies and bike tools for emergencies.
   My worst experiences have been *crashes,* but slowing for danger and protective gear have saved me a lot of pain. Most crashes don't cause serious injury. A helmet, full-finger leather gloves, over-the-ankle boots, long pants, long sleeves and dark glasses have saved me many times from scrapes and painful impacts with rocks, dirt, and brush.
   Maintain full control of your bike at all times, watching for excess speed and over-heated brakes on steep downhills. Showing respect for the environment and other trail users will ensure more enjoyment for yourself, and also help ensure continued access to this beautiful backcountry.

Harmful Animals and Plants: Several plants and animals here are potentially harmful. It helps to know what to avoid and how to handle encounters.
   Black bears are out and about, and although I have never been bothered by them and seldom see them, they are much larger than I am. Food seems to cause the most bear problems, so a clean camp is advised.
   Rattlesnakes can be startling and are dangerous at close range, but they are usually noisy and retreat readily. Snakes are most often seen during periods of hot weather.
   Tarantulas are sometimes seen, but they are intent on going their own way and soon disappear.
   Scorpions can be found under some rocks and loose tree bark. I have seen only two or three, but then I don't go looking for them. The scorpions in

this area have a sting that is toxic to some people, although I have never heard of their bothering anyone.

Ticks are most numerous during the rainy season, but they can be encountered all year — mostly in thick brush. Watch for them on your clothing and brush them off. (It helps to wear light-colored clothing.) If a tick bites you, remove it as soon as possible. It can sometimes be persuaded to let go if you pass a hot coal or a burning match nearby. Another trick is to apply Vaseline, oil, or grease over them so they let go to avoid smothering. If all that fails, I just pull it off with a twisting motion, slowly, and using a disinfectant ointment. These are most unpleasant little crawly things. Dogs are bothered more by ticks than people are, but they will abandon a dog in water. I've had three bites in 30 years. I hope that's all, but they aren't going to keep me out of the forest.

Scrub oak, live oak, and holly leaves all have small, sharp thorns on their edges, while other species of brush have longer, sharp thorns on the branches. On trails and especially overgrown sections, protective clothing will prevent a lot of annoying, small cuts and scrapes. A much more dangerous plant that grows along the trails is yucca. It looks like a clump of pale green spear points about 10" long that guarantee respect. A skin puncture near a joint (elbow, knee, etc.) can cause some stiffness and lack of flexibility for a while.

Poison oak should be avoided. This three-leaved plant — sometimes a bush and other times vine-like — has an oil that causes rashes with blistering one to five days after contact. Direct contact with any part of the plant, contact with an animal that has brushed against it, contact with clothing or gloves that have touched it, or inhalation of smoke from a burning plant can cause the rash. Washing immediately can prevent or lessen the rash. Derma-Pax itch-relieving lotion by Recsei Labs, in Goleta, California, is sold over-the-counter and is my choice for poison oak. More severe cases require medical care. Extremely sensitive people might check with a doctor about having desensitizing shots or drops.

Horses and Pack Animals: Many of the trails in Ventura County are used by recreational horse riders. Some horses are spooked easily, so make them aware of your presence *well in advance of the encounter.*

• If you come upon horses moving *toward* you, yield the right-of-way, even if it seems inconvenient. Carry your bike to the downhill side and stand quietly, well off the trail in a spot where the animals can see you clearly. A startled horse can cause serious injuries both to an inexperienced rider and to itself.

• If you come upon horses *moving ahead of you in the same direction*, stop well behind them. Do not attempt to pass until you have alerted the riders and asked for permission. Then, pass as quietly as you can on the downhill side of the trail, well below the horses.

• It is your responsibility to ensure that such encounters are safe for everyone.

Trailside Bike Repair: Minimum equipment: pump, spare tube, patches, 2 tubes of patch glue, 6" adjustable wrench, Allen wrenches, chain tool, spoke wrench, and spare axle. (Tools may be shared with others in your group.)

Correct inflation, wide tires, and avoiding rocks will prevent most flats. Those same rocks cause bent and broken axles. Grease, oil, and proper adjustment will prevent almost all mechanical failures. Frequent stream crossings wash out chain grease; carry extra or — if worse comes to worst — use a banana peel like we have had to do!

Overnight Tours: The longer the trip, the more things you should take. On a short one-day trip, little is needed. Longer day trips require food, extra water, possible clothing changes, and bike repair items.

Overnight mountain bike touring can take on the look of an expedition. The mountain bicycle's robust parts and low gearing make it possible to pack and carry heavy loads. This is no problem touring on good, level roads. However, riding uphill, dodging rocks, and descending steep slopes is much more difficult with heavy loads and unstable bags.

Pushing becomes a frequent, hated chore, and carrying a hard-to-balance, loaded mountain bike over, through, and around obstacles is exhausting work. Most camping equipment does not provide enough camp comfort to make up for the effort it takes you to carry it there and back.

I drink lots of water the day before a trip, just before starting out, and every place I refill my water bottles. It's like having an extra water bottle. During hot, dry trips I carry additional water in reused 2-liter plastic soda bottles.

Take lots of food, including snacks for en route. Dry foods such as rice, cereal, potato flakes, pasta or commercial pre-packaged dry meals are best unless you're dry camping, in which case you might as well carry hydrated food. I cook over wood fires using one aluminum pot with a lid and one spoon that I also eat with. Los Padres National Forest has an abundance of wood available. Check with the Los Padres Forest Service for current fire regulations for the area you plan to visit. During fire restrictions it's cold food for your menu. The weather is so hot when that happens that cold food is generally not a problem.

A tent is seldom needed, as summer rain is rare; the area often goes eight months at a time without rain. I use a plastic ground cloth, a 1/2" foam pad, and a winter or summer sleeping bag with a piece of netting pulled over my head to keep the bugs away.

Navigation: It's easy to get lost. Have a plan ready in advance with your group in case you lose your way. Before you leave on your trip, tell someone where you're going, when you expect to return, and what to do in case you don't return on time. When you are more than six hours overdue ask them to call the Ventura County Sheriff, giving full details about your vehicle and your trip plans.

En route, keep track of your position on your trip map(s); record the

times you arrive at known places on the map. The maps in this volume are designed as an aid only, to help you find the right starting points or to interpret official maps.

Carry and consult the high-quality topo maps, preferably the new USGS 7.5 minute series and Fine Edge Productions's Ventura County Map. The USFS map is also helpful. *Warning: There are numerous errors in the published data of the Coast Range, and you need to check and make comparisons between maps.* USGS 15-minute topographical maps are old and outdated with regard to man-made features such roads and trails.

Occasionally, you may not know where you are. Be sure to look back frequently in the direction from which you came, in case you need to retrace your path. *Do not be afraid to turn back when conditions change or the going is rougher than you expected.*

If you have arranged to meet someone, allow enough time. It frequently takes both parties longer to rendez-vous than expected. Meet at a road intersection that cannot be confused by either party. (It's difficult to locate someone in a large campground!) Write down instructions for both parties before you leave.

In certain cases, it may be difficult to determine which roads and trails are open to public travel. When in doubt, make local inquiries. Follow signs and leave all gates either opened or closed (as you found them) or as signed. Park off the road, even in remote areas, so you do not block possible emergency vehicles. *Avoid solo travel in remote areas.*

Mileages: Many of the mileages given in this book are one-way mileages for a single trail; they do not reflect the total mileage of a loop or out-and-back trip.

In this book we refer to highway mileage markers to help locate junctions, parking areas, trailheads and emergency services. Many of the white vertical road reflectors have these mileages printed on them in black numbers. State Highway 33 is numbered from 0.00 at U.S. 101 in Ventura. The marker on Highway 33 at Rose Valley Road turnoff reads 25.84, which means Rose Valley Road is that distance from U.S. 101 in Ventura via Highway 33. If you're at a junction of Highway 33 and a dirt road heading east, and the mileage marker indicates 28.07, Rose Valley Road is 2.23 miles closer to Ventura than you are.

The authors, illustrators, photographers and publisher accept no responsibility for inaccuracies or for damages incurred while attempting any routes listed in this book.

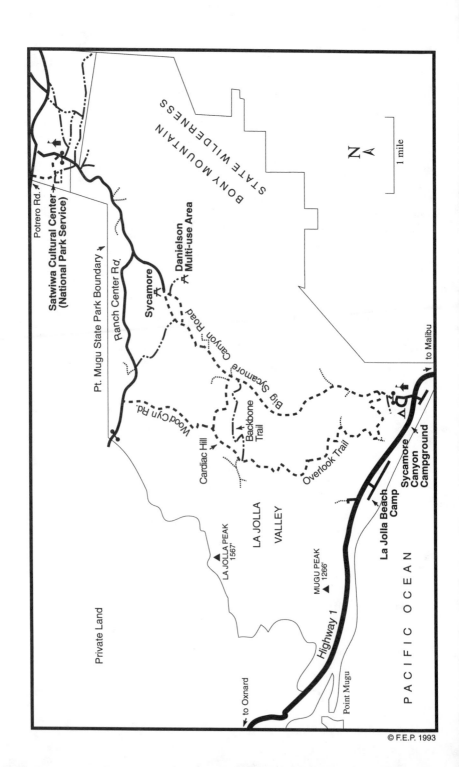

Satwiwa Cultural Center
(National Park Service)

Potrero Rd.

Pt. Mugu State Park Boundary

Ranch Center Rd.

Sycamore

BONY MOUNTAIN STATE WILDERNESS

Danielson
Multi-use Area

Big Sycamore Canyon Road

Wood Cyn Rd.

Cardiac Hill

Backbone
Trail

Overlook Trail

Private Land

LA JOLLA PEAK
1567'

LA JOLLA
VALLEY

MUGU PEAK
1266'

Highway 1

La Jolla Beach
Camp

Sycamore
Canyon
Campground

to Malibu

to Oxnard

Point Mugu

PACIFIC OCEAN

N

1 mile

© F.E.P. 1993

CHAPTER 1   POINT MUGU STATE PARK
Big Sycamore Canyon, Overlook Trail, Wood Canyon Trail

The Santa Monica Mountain Range to the northwest of Los Angeles, with its spectacular vistas, rugged backcountry and protected park areas, is an excellent refuge for those seeking to escape urban sprawl and city hustle. Point Mugu State Park lies along the western edge of this mountain range in Ventura County and has preserved some of the finest and most diverse sections of this terrain. Included in its 13,000 acres, you can find five miles of ocean shoreline, rocky bluffs, sandy beaches, windblown sand dunes, and a backcountry with rugged peaks, deep canyons, large groves of trees and pastoral grasslands. A number of dirt trails and roads wind through this area and provide excellent mountain bike riding. Inland valley summers may be hot and dry with 100 degree temperatures common, but here, tall sycamore trees provide welcome shade, and along the beach, where salt air blows cool, you can walk barefoot in the surf in a water temperature that seldom rises above 65 degrees.

An observation platform, located on the west side of Highway 101 four miles northwest of Sycamore Cove, overlooks the saltwater Mugu Lagoon. There is a picnic table here, and it's a good place to watch for birds or take a rest if you're heading up the coast on a bike trip. Point Mugu Rock, a popular bouldering area for climbers, is located one mile to the southeast. From the observation platform you can see several rare or endangered birds. These include the brown pelican, the light footed clapper rail, belding savannah sparrow, California least tern and salt marsh birds beak. To the east of the lagoon grows the giant coreopsis plant, which blooms bright yellow on the coastal bluffs and sea terraces in the spring. Please do not disturb these birds or plants; they are protected species. *Note:* The land behind the fence is government property, and unauthorized persons must stay out.

Early History

Point Mugu State Park takes its name from the Chumash word *muwu,* which means beach. From the coastal end of the Santa Monica Mountains, north and west for 100 miles or more, lived one of the more advanced and peaceful groups of the North American Indians. The Chumash culture had existed for 6000 years before European man arrived, and when Juan Rodriguez Cabrillo dropped anchor off the Pacific Coast in October 1542, he was amazed to find such an advanced people. The Chumash, who could paddle their lightweight planked canoes in circles around the slow sailing ships, were perhaps the first culture to go technologically beyond the heavy dug-out log canoes.

As you pedal your lightweight mountain bike in the Ventura backcountry you will pass many Chumash sites, including caves with beautifully colored wall paintings. Concern for their survival won't allow us to pinpoint the locations of these caves. However, if you truly appreciate Native American values and can duplicate those natural instincts for survival and beauty, you will undoubtedly discover these sites on your own. Show your respect: "Take nothing but pictures and leave nothing but footprints."

Within Point Mugu State Park the observant cyclist or hiker can find many species of wildlife in varied habitats. Majestic golden eagles are seen along with the endangered pelican and numerous other birds. Large clusters of monarch butterflies winter here. You may find mule deer, rabbits, gray fox, skunks, badgers and coyotes; even bobcats and mountain lions can be seen on occasion. From the bluffs, such as those on Overlook Trail, you can see dolphins and migrating California grey whales as they travel along the coast.

Getting to Point Mugu State Park

You may enter this part of the Santa Monica Mountains from the Ventura Freeway (101) at Newbury Park by taking Borchard Road south to Reino Road, then going right on Potrero Road to the signed entrance to Rancho Sierra Vista/ Satwiwa Park. The northern entrance is under the jurisdiction of the National Park Service. Its 500 acres are adjacent to the north end of Big Sycamore Canyon and Point Mugu State Park, whose 13,000 acres spread all the way to

the ocean. You may park for free by turning left (east) from Reino Road onto Potrero Road and using the trailhead lot about 1/4 mile east near Wendy Drive.

Most bicyclists enter the park from the Pacific Coast Highway, Route 1, at Point Mugu State Park Head-quarters near the mouth of Big Sycamore Canyon. The road into the park is well marked by signs along the highway. By starting near the ocean, all the roads and trails are uphill, and tired riders appreciate the downhill return.

Parking: A day use parking lot is available in the park, 8:00 a.m. to dusk, $6 per day. Turn left just past the entrance kiosk where the ranger will collect the fee. If the ranger is out you must use the self pay "Iron Ranger" as the signs direct. Maps are also for sale for 75¢ from a dispenser. Free parking is available alongside the highway, both east and west of the park, 10:00 a.m. to 5:00 p.m. The preferred parking beside this busy highway is on the north side (so you don't have to cross the road), but keep away from the cliffs where falling rocks would damage your vehicle.

Camping: Sycamore Canyon Campground—51 spaces, $14 per day, $6 extra vehicle, $3 per person hike and bike, hot showers available. La Jolla State Beach Camp—101 spaces on the beach 1/2 mile west of Big Sycamore Canyon. To make reservations for either campground, call 1-800-444-PARK.

Water: At Sycamore Campground and Danielson Multi-use Area.

Nearest Services: Emergency phones are located at Sycamore Campground, Danielson Multi-use Area, and the Ranch Center in Wood Canyon. Dial 911.

Big Sycamore Canyon Road
Length: 8 miles
Level of Difficulty: Easy if you ride from the beach; there is one very steep climb at the north end of the canyon.
Elevation: Sea level to 800'

Long and deep, Big Sycamore Canyon cuts through the length of the park between steep-sided mountains, especially the 3111-foot Bony Mountain on the east. For 6 miles you can ride up the nearly level canyon passing under sycamore trees and stopping to rest at picnic areas in the shade of huge spreading live oaks. After passing through narrow parts of the canyon the large pastoral meadows are a pleasant surprise. Lingering here in the quiet of the canyon where little has changed for centuries, you can get an understanding of the peaceful ways of the Chumash people. All of the other roads and trails open to bicycles branch off to the west from this main road.

As you enter Big Sycamore Canyon from Highway 1 and pass by the campground information and fee station, the day use parking lot is to your left. A restroom is located next to the south lot, and water is available there. Ride through the campground on the paved one-way road following the counterclockwise traffic flow. Big Sycamore Canyon Road starts at a locked gate on the north end of the campground beside the paved loop road. Pass by the right side of the gate and head north on this dirt road. A bicycle safety sign with important park information and special rules is directly ahead on your right. This is a heavy use area, and you must yield to all hikers and equestrians.

You may top off your water bottles from a faucet mounted on a fire hydrant on the left side of the road at mile 0.4. The Overlook Trail (double-track) branches off to the west just past the hydrant at mile 0.42. By looking left beyond the usually dry stream and up through the trees, you can see the Overlook Trail climbing up the steep canyon side to the west. That trail requires much more stamina and bicycle handling skill than the easy dirt road up Big Sycamore Canyon. Through most of the canyon the bottom is flat, from side to side between steep chaparral covered slopes, The stream has cut a meandering gulch 5- to 10-feet-deep that the road crosses repeatedly; it is your greatest challenge. The trick is to keep your momentum without hitting a rock or rut left by the water flow.

A single-track trail (no bicycles) starts on the left at mile 0.8 and climbs to join the Overlook Trail. After crossing the creek again you pass the Serano Trail on the right at 1.08 miles. It heads east into the Bony Mountain Wilderness and is also closed to bicycles. Past here the canyon turns to the west and enters a more narrow section where there are more oak and black walnut trees. When you complete the "S" turn and are headed north again, there are two tables under a huge spreading oak on the left at 1.98 miles.

After more creek crossings you pass a segment of the Backbone Trail on the left (west) that climbs 1.8 miles to the Overlook Trail. This part is open to bicycles on an experimental basis. Most riders prefer to ride up the roads and return down this steep single-track trail (see description below). After more creek crossings you come to the junction of Wood Canyon Road at 3.0 miles. If you take this trail, it will lead you northwest to the Ranch Center or up Cardiac Hill to the Overlook Trail.

Keep right in Big Sycamore Canyon and you pass to the right of a large meadow. After crossing to the west side of the creek, you come to a crossroads with a power line road heading west and the east road crossing a field to the Danielson Multi-use Area. If you keep on straight ahead there is another creek crossing, and at 4.6 miles the dirt road ends. Turn left here onto the paved section of Sycamore Canyon Road to continue north up the canyon.

The Danielson Multi-use Area is 0.2 mile to the right on the paved road. There are picnic tables among the oaks, a large group barbecue, piped water, and restrooms with a phone at the east end.

Go back up to where you came to the paved road, continue north, and at 5 miles from Sycamore Camp there is another picnic area with portable toilets on the right and tables on the left. Just ahead on the left are some pipe horse corrals. At 5.5 miles the paved Ranch Center Road is to the west (left). (You can take that road over a steep hill to the Ranch Center and return down Wood Canyon.)

This junction is a good turn-around point because if you continue north on Sycamore Canyon Road you will be climbing a very steep hill. Those who come in from the north will know what that have to face getting back. The rest of us can just turn back.

Ranch Center Road
Length: 2.3 miles
Level of Difficulty: Moderate; although paved there is a very steep hill on both sides of the ridge
Elevation: 400' - 700'; 300' diff.

Take Big Sycamore Canyon Road described above to get to the start of Ranch

Center Road. It starts down a little, crossing a bridge and then a couple of small hills. At 0.4 mile you will have no doubt about where the big hill is, and it's up steeply for 1.2 miles followed by a little more climbing to traverse to the west. Soon, at 1.9 miles, there is a saddle and a large water tank to the left. Then it's downhill to the Ranch Center at 2.3 miles. There is a public phone there on the side of a large shed-like barn. Wood Canyon Road continues on to the south from the Center by passing to the east of a mobile home surrounded by a high chain-link fence.

Wood Canyon Road

Length: 2.7 miles
Level of Difficulty: Moderate. This is a rough double-track where it is very important to be in total control of your speed.
Elevation: 200' - 475'; 275' diff.
Caution: There are many steep stream crossings where the water has washed away the soil from around the pipe culverts and left them half exposed in the bottom of the crossings.

Wood Canyon is much narrower and has a steeper grade than Big Sycamore Canyon There are fewer sycamore trees, but it is thick with oaks. It is all downhill from the Ranch Center except for climbing out of creek crossings. At 1.7 miles there are picnic tables on the right and you are at the junction where the road up to the saddle overlooking La Jolla Valley starts on the right. It's so steep as to be called Cardiac Hill. Wood Canyon turns to the southeast here and travels another mile to where it joins into Big Sycamore Canyon.

From Sycamore Camp up Big Sycamore Canyon Road, across on Ranch Center Road, down Wood Canyon and return to Sycamore Camp is 13.5 miles.

Overlook Trail

Length: 4.5 miles
Level of Difficulty: Moderate. The park calls this route a trail, yet the ranger can drive a pickup truck over it with ease. This "trail" has some steep parts, a long grade, and a few bothersome rocks and ruts.
Elevation: 50' - 1200'; 1150' diff.

The Overlook Trail is a much more challenging ride than the roads that wind along the bottom of the canyons in the park. You climb 1150 feet, descend some steep places over rocks and ruts, and ride long stretches where the mountain drops away from the roadside for hundreds of feet. Traveling on the ridge-top between Big Sycamore Canyon and La Jolla Valley you can see out over most of the area and get an appreciation of the unique character and location of Point Mugu State Park. During clear weather you can see Catalina and the Channel Islands, and small boats and big ships leave disappearing tracks across the sea. Thousands of gray whales migrate past here every winter, and the "overlook"

above the Coast Highway is one of the best places to spot them from land.

I prefer to ride the Overlook as a 9.3-mile counter-clockwise loop. Ride up Big Sycamore Canyon Road 3 miles, turn left onto Wood Canyon Road and go 3/4 mile to Deer Camp Junction. Turn left and climb the very steep Cardiac Hill, 3/4 mile and 600 feet up to the saddle where you can look across La Jolla Valley. The road into the valley past this saddle is closed to bicycles. The Overlook Trail starts from the saddle and heads directly south (left).

You climb 100 yards and on the left you pass the upper end of a segment of the Backbone Trail that is the only single-track trail open to bicycles in the park. Climb steeply again and at 0.25 mile you level out some to pass a road at 0.33 mile. (It goes up to a water tank on the left.) Then you ride on the ridge through a dip with views on both sides. There's more climbing, and at 0.8 mile the road circles to the east of a 1221-foot peak. Cross a saddle with another good view into La Jolla Valley to the west, dip down a little, and at the next saddle (1.26 miles) you have the first good view of the ocean.

The next 3 miles make up a long descent, most of it an easy grade, but some moderately steep sections require caution. The Backbone Trail, which starts at the Ray Miller Trailhead way below in La Jolla Canyon, joins the Overlook Trail at 2.5 miles. At 3.6 miles there is a sharp turn to the east, and here a foot trail (closed to bicycles) heads south to the "overlook" this trail is named for. On that trail you can look down on the great sand dune next to the highway.

Descending to the east you enter a series of steep switchbacks that take you into the bottom of Big Sycamore Canyon. Cross the creek and turn right onto the road back to camp and the highway.

Backbone Trail (from Overlook Trail to Sycamore Canyon)
Length: 1.8 miles
Level of Difficulty: More difficult; this is a true single-track trail and is narrow and steep with sharp switchbacks
Elevation: 200' - 950'; 750' diff.

Most people ride this from the top down by taking Big Sycamore Canyon Road to Wood Canyon Road and up Cardiac Hill to the Overlook Trail (see other ride descriptions in this chapter). From the Overlook Trail, turn left on to the signed Backbone Trail and ride out on the ridge to the east. This is a good, much-used trail. Be careful to make the turn to the left at the first switchback. You follow the ridge down to the east, except where it gets too steep, and then you zigzag down the mountain. You come out onto Big Sycamore Canyon Road 0.3 mile south of the Wood Canyon junction.

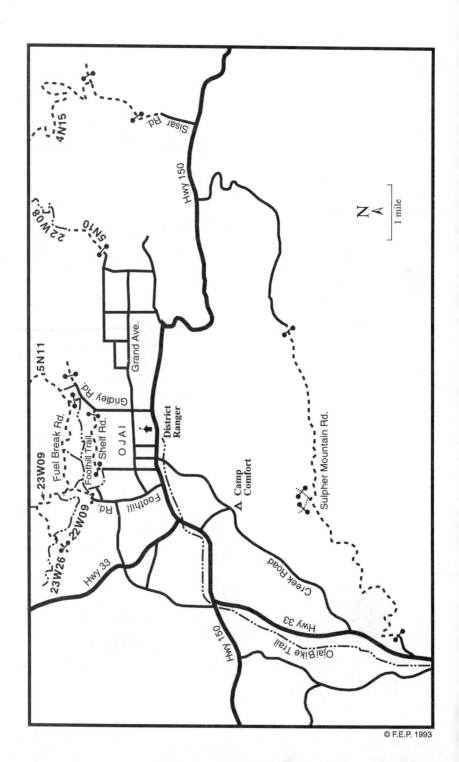

N

1 mile

4N15

Sisar Rd.

Hwy 150

22W08

5N10

Grand Ave.

5N11

Gridley Rd.

Fuel Break Rd.

District Ranger

Foothill Trail

Shelf Rd.

O J A I

23W09

2W09

Foothill Rd.

Camp Comfort

Sulpher Mountain Rd.

23W26

Hwy 33

Creek Road

Hwy 33

Hwy 150

Ojai Bike Trail

© F.E.P. 1993

CHAPTER 2   OJAI VALLEY
Sulphur Mountain Road, Shelf Road, Fuel Break Road, Foothill Trail, Cozy Dell Road, Cozy Dell Trail

For cyclists Ojai has it all. Surrounded by mountains, Ojai Valley offers mountain views from every point. Rural roads pass through orange groves and under spreading oaks, and a new bike path following the old railroad bed provides opportunities for the road cyclist to explore the valley at an unhurried pace. Challenging mountain highways are used by local riders for training and racing; some of these riders have gone on to Olympic medals and professional careers.

As either a destination or a starting point, Ojai Valley is a gateway for mountain biking. Everything a mountain biker needs you can find here. Food, lodging, supplies, hospital (hopefully not needed), ranger and sheriff stations, bike shops, entertainment and — in a place noted for its tennis tournament — lots of tennis courts. Stores, motels and resort hotels, golf courses and campgrounds provide a good base for non-riding family members who can entertain themselves while others are out enjoying the trails.

Winter rains in January and February may make riding something to dream about, but the rest of the year is fine. However, some summer days can be so hot that riding *only* in early morning is advised. Unless you are used to extreme heat, don't ride in the noon sun. Most of the local rides are short and close to town, so a bike is transportation enough. Longer day rides are possible, especially if there is a driver who can drop you off so you can ride back over the mountain to Ojai.

Sulphur Mountain Road
Route/Trail: No number
Length: 9-mile dirt road
Level of Difficulty: Easy
Elevation: 300' - 2600'
Water: None
Parking: At turn-out on Sulphur Mountain Road and Highway 33 (mile marker 7.40). Do not park by the locked gate and block the way.
Campgrounds: None
Nearest Services: Ojai

Between Casitas Springs and San Antonio Creek Bridge, turn right off Highway 33 onto Sulphur Mountain Road. Travel east on the paved road past the Girl Scout Camp on the left to a locked gate. Sulphur Mountain Road is a county road, dirt and gravel graded, and it's open to foot traffic, bicycles and horses. It is closed to traffic/motor vehicles except those driven by local property owners and employees of Edison Company and Ventura County. Side roads and off-road property are posted "no trespassing"; you must stay on the road.

There is about 9 miles of dirt road, which travels from Highway 33 to Highway 150 in a northeasterly direction. It is mostly uphill from the east end at 300' above sea level to 2600' at the highest point near the west end of the road. An oil spring 100 yards up from the gate is a messy, unusual road hazard.

I generally go in Sulphur Mountain Road from the east end, ride up first, then return the same way I came. The first climb is steep, but it soon levels out after about 1.5 miles. Then there is mostly steady climbing the rest of the way. Often there are cattle — including large bulls — on the road. Slow travel and patience is the best way to get past them. Give them time, and they'll usually get off the road. If they don't move, don't run them or chase them; just keep moving slowly. *Close all gates you open.*

This ride is good all year except just after a rainstorm, when it can be muddy. The views are exceptional mountain vistas to the north and Lake Casitas to the west. As the road goes on and up to the top, you have views of Topa Topa Bluff,

Sisar Canyon and Santa Paula Peak. The southern view, after your initial climb out of Ventura River Canyon, looks across Cañada Larga to Ventura, Oxnard and the Pacific Ocean. On clear days, you can see several of the Channel Islands — Anacapa, Santa Cruz and Santa Rosa. There are even exceptional days of Santa Ana northeast winds when you can see all seven of the coastal islands, including Catalina.

The land in this area is covered mainly with grasses, live oak trees and some sage. It's quite green in the early spring with plenty of wildflowers. Later, it becomes very dry and brown. Those who travel silently and watch carefully may see wildlife: coyotes, bobcats, deer, quail, hawks, snakes and small birds.

I "share" this road with you in the hopes we and our children may be able to ride it the rest of our days. In years past, I drove it in passenger cars when it was a popular Sunday drive. Later, when 4WD and motorcycle traffic activities got out of hand, vehicle travel was no longer allowed. Please be considerate of other trail users and use good cycling judgment to help preserve our good fortune.

This ride may be part of a loop by continuing to paved Highway 150 and Upper Ojai, or by continuing to Sisar Canyon for more mountain riding.

Shelf Road
Route/Trail: No number
Length: 1.75 miles
Level of Difficulty: Easy, beginner
Elevation: 1000'
Water: None
Parking: Along Signal Street, Grand Avenue, or near your favorite restaurant or ice cream shop
Campgrounds: None
Nearest Services: Ojai

A short, easy dirt road that's 1.75 miles long, Shelf Road is a public route closed to motor traffic and gated at each end. It runs east and west at the north edge of town between Signal Street and Gridley Road. Follow Signal Street uphill to its end, bearing slightly right past a white gate. Stay on the main dirt road and watch for walkers, runners and horseback riders.

This delightful road climbs and descends less than 200', keeping most of the time around the 1000' elevation contour. You have views of the east end of Ojai, and the steep slopes put you right above some residences. Riding in summer is best done in early morning or late afternoon. Or how about a sunrise ride before breakfast? You can make this a loop ride, connecting back along Grand Avenue or return back along Shelf Road again. One way takes about 30 minutes with enough time to look at the scenery. Meditative rides will take much longer, but it's time well spent.

Fuel Break Road

Route/Trail: No number
Length: 2.3 miles, from Gridley Road to Stewart Canyon/Pratt Trail Road
Level of Difficulty: Moderate; trail access is very rough and steep
Elevation: 1200' - 1800'; 600' diff.
Water: None
Parking: End of Gridley Road; Stewart Canyon Debris Dam
Campgrounds: None
Nearest Services: Ojai

A wide fuel break has been cut along the south side of Nordhoff Peak between Gridley Canyon and Stewart Canyon. For firefighting and maintenance purposes, a fire road was built along this fuel break. It is a good, graded road with excellent views of the Ojai Valley and no long hills to climb. Its closeness to town makes it a popular training ride.

For this ride, the best access is at the upper end of Gridley Road. Just below the turnaround ride and walk north on the signed Gridley Connector Trail #22W05. You climb steeply a short way to Gridley Road #5N11. Turn left and travel downhill 1/3 mile and take Fuel Break Road on the right uphill toward the west. Here you will be alternately climbing and descending to the west and then dropping into Stewart Canyon. At the junction with Pratt Trail #23W09 you may turn left and travel down the canyon and come out at the Stewart Canyon Debris Dam. There is parking for trail users there. From there you may loop back to Gridley by way of Shelf Road. (Street access to the debris dam from Ojai is by traveling north on Signal to very near the end at Shelf Road; turn left by a very large water tank, and within 100 yards you will see the dam.)

You may also travel up the Pratt Trail from the Fuel Break Road by turning right and heading up the canyon on a road that takes you up on the ridge between Stewart Canyon and Cozy Dell Canyon. On that ridge the Pratt Trail branches off and climbs on up the mountain; the road there doubles back and drops down into Cozy Dell Canyon (see the Cozy Dell Road ride).

Foothill Trail

Route/Trail: #22W09
Length: 3.4 miles from Gridley Road to Cozy Dell Canyon
Level of Difficulty: Expert only — trials courses are easy after this one!
Elevation: 1200' - 1700'; 500' diff.
Water: None
Parking: Along Gridley Road or Foothill Road. If you do it as a loop, park in Ojai (Grand Ave.).
Campgrounds: None
Nearest Services: Ojai

The foothills between Ojai Valley and Nordhoff Peak are a series of parallel east-west ridges cut by canyons from above. These ridges are like knife edges, very steep towards Ojai Valley; the side away from the valley is so steep in places as to be cliffs. Foothill Trail runs parallel to these ridges, and sometimes in between them, hidden from Ojai Valley. In other places, it crosses over to the Ojai Valley side, affording a special view of the valley.

This trail, in many places, is the same as when my friends and I rode it in the late 1950s after school, and in the summer as a training ride to keep in shape. Now almost 30 years later, we ride it after work in the summer on bikes with two-wheel brakes and 18 speeds, marveling at how well we used to do with single speed, one-wheel brakes. The frames aren't that much different, and the wheels and tires are still the same size.

Make no mistake — this is one rough trail. Plan to do a loop trip, so you don't have to do any part twice, while it's still fresh in your mind and body. I believe the worst part is from Gridley Road to Foothill Road and Pratt Trail.

Start by going up paved Gridley Road from Grand Avenue. Gridley Road turns right and crosses a bridge, then straightens out, climbs steeply and turns right again. At this point, take the potholed, paved road to the left. Fifty yards along this road to the left is a water well and a pump with a tank, an iron gate and no fence, and a series of 2-foot-high barrier rocks along the roadside. Directly west of these rocks is the beginning of Foothill Trail #22W09, unsigned at this time.

From this trailhead to the ridge top 1/2 mile away, the trail is very rocky, with 6" x 8" wooden waterstops all along. This section is mostly push-and-carry. At first Ojai Valley is not visible, but soon the trail crosses a saddle and the valley is spread out below. From this point, the trail descends and climbs for about 1/3 mile to a second overlook. Next, you have a half-mile, mostly rideable descent into a canyon. Ride up the other side, and at 1.45 miles from the start, there is a trail to the right that climbs up the ridge above the canyon you just passed. This trail connects to Fuel Break Road, which parallels the Foothill Trail (see the previous ride description). At 1.65 miles, you top out onto another saddle and then it's a sometimes rough descent to Stewart Canyon, Pratt Trail/Road #23W09. This part of the Pratt Trail is a road from the mouth of Stewart Canyon past Fuel Break Road and up on the west side of the canyon connecting to Cozy Dell Canyon. Total distance from Gridley Road to Pratt Trail is 2.0 miles.

If you're still game, instead of heading back to Ojai you can turn uphill on Pratt Trail/Road, go 0.2 mile, and turn left at the signed Foothill Trail. Go down canyon until Foothill Trail branches right. From there, it switchbacks, west up out of Stewart Canyon. The trail climbs, descends and climbs a short way again for almost 1 mile to the high point before descending into Cozy Dell Canyon. You come out onto Cozy Dell Canyon Road 1.36 miles from Pratt Trail.

From this point, you may turn uphill on Cozy Dell Road and climb 1.75 miles to connect with Pratt Trail #23W09 and return down to Foothill Road and Ojai. Or from the same point go left down Cozy Dell Road about 100 feet and look to the right for signed Trail #23W26, which leads 2 miles to Highway 33.

Cozy Dell Road
Route/Trail: No number
Length: 2 miles
Level of Difficulty: Moderate; steep climb
Elevation: 1400' - 2080'; 680' diff.
Water: None
Parking: Stewart Canyon Debris Dam
Campgrounds: None
Nearest Services: Ojai

This is a nice ride in the canyon past oak trees that shade the road. Cozy Dell Road — a continuation of Fuel Break and Pratt Trail roads — drops down Cozy Dell Canyon from Pratt Trail #23W09 and heads out to a gate at the ranch in the mouth of the canyon.

Start by turning off the north end of Signal Street near a large water tank and heading west to the Stewart Canyon Debris Dam. If you are driving, park in the space provided near the corrals. Take signed Pratt Trail up the canyon here, passing many residences. There are twists and turns to the trail before you finally get beyond the homes to the dirt road section of Pratt Trail. Continue up the canyon past Foothill Trail #22W09 and Fuel Break Road, both to your right. Continue climbing until the road crosses the ridge on the west side of Stewart Canyon.

Cozy Dell Road begins at the saddle; take it west and downhill. At the next fork go right, down into the canyon. (The left fork climbs up to the ridge and ends.) At the bottom of this side canyon there is a road heading into upper Cozy Dell Canyon to dead-end at some water works. Ignore this and continue left and down past Foothill Trail on the left. About 100 feet farther on the right you'll find Cozy Dell Trail #23W26, which leads to Highway 33. (If you continue on Cozy Dell Road about 1/2 mile, you'll reach the locked gate of Cozy Dell Ranch. Do not pass this point.)

Cozy Dell Trail
Route/Trail: #23W26
Length: 2 miles; Highway 33 to Cozy Dell Canyon Road
Level of Difficulty: Very difficult; rocky; a lot of poison oak
Elevation: 960' - 1560'; 600' diff.
Water: None
Parking: At the turnout south of Friends Ranch orange store
Campgrounds: None
Nearest Services: Ojai

Beginning at Highway 33's mile post 14.57 just south of a concrete bridge, Cozy Dell Trail drops into the creek bed for a short distance and then climbs the right (south) side of the canyon. This section is very rocky with many switchbacks. Poison oak is plentiful here, so beware. After climbing to a ridge top, the trail drops and then climbs again before descending into Cozy Dell Canyon to join Cozy Dell Road.

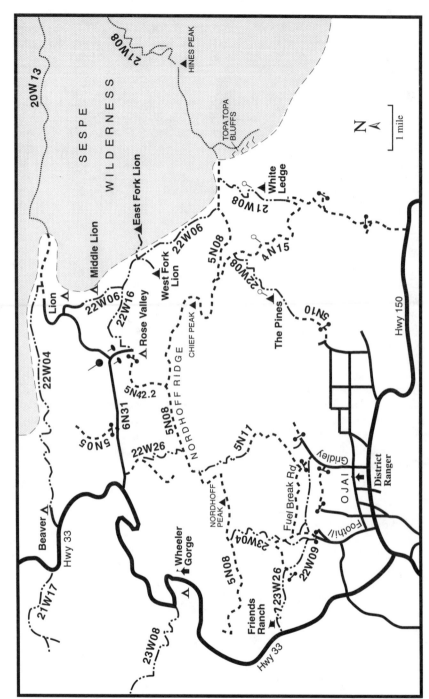

© F.E.P. 1993

CHAPTER 3   NORDHOFF RIDGE
Nordhoff Ridge, Gridley Trail, Sisar Canyon/Red Reef Trail,
Sisar Canyon Road, Chief Peak Road, Howard Canyon Trail

Rising abruptly out of Matilija Creek and climbing 12 miles to the east to Topa Topa Bluffs, Nordhoff Ridge separates Ojai Valley and Sespe Canyon. This 50-square-mile area is characterized by steep, narrow canyons and even steeper ridges. The chaparral-covered sloping terrain contains only small streams and in summer most of these dry up. Water can usually be found at springs and where canyons are the steepest and narrowest and the water is flowing over bedrock. In winter, snow occurs above 3,000 feet. Rainfall can be very heavy in storms that last three to four days, and streams become raging torrents that are extremely dangerous. Nordhoff Ridge receives an average rainfall of 28 inches a year, about twice that of Ojai Valley just 5 miles away. Most of this rain occurs during January, February, and March.

The vistas from Nordhoff Ridge are spectacular: you see Ojai Valley, the Pacific Ocean and Channel Islands to the south, and to the north are peaks and ridges separated by deep canyons across the Sespe Wilderness. A fire road travels the length of Nordhoff Ridge. Roads and trails switchback up out of the lateral canyons and ridges from Ojai Valley on the south and Rose Valley to the north. The shortest way to the ridge is by Chief Peak Road #5N42.2 from Rose Valley.

Possible rides here are up-and-backs, traverses, and loop trips. Three trail camps provide limited camping opportunities. West Fork Lion Canyon, The Pines, and White Ledge trail camps are all located near year-round water sources. Gridley Spring trail camp was washed away by flood water, but there is a plan to relocate it nearby with volunteer labor. Campgrounds accessible by automobile are Wheeler Gorge on Highway 33 and Rose Valley, Middle Lion, and Lion camps along paved Rose Valley Road.

Nordhoff Ridge
Route/Trail: Road #5N08
Length: 17 miles
Level of Difficulty: Moderate; some sections very strenuous
Elevation: 2,500' - 5,500'
Water: None
Access: Up lateral trails and roads; access is blocked at Wheeler Springs
Campgrounds: Unimproved sites only
Nearest Services: Ojai

This east-west ridge, with a very good fire road running its length and on to Topa Topa Bluff, offers the best riding in the area. The views are spectacular. The entire road is rideable and much of it is a moderate grade. The only water to be found on the ridge is at stock ponds — water you must *not* drink. Trail camps no longer exist on the ridge, but many excellent (unimproved) camping locations are available. No fires are allowed during fire season, which is generally July to December, depending on rainfall. A yearly fire permit is required and is available at most U.S. Forest Service Stations. Check for current conditions. I have broken Road #5N08 into sections below for ease of riding.

A. El Camino Cielo — Nordhoff Peak to Wheeler Hot Springs
Route/Trail: Road #5N08
Length: 4 miles one way
Level of Difficulty: Very strenuous, and it's a long way back
Elevation: 4,477' - 2,500'; 1,977' descent that must be climbed to return (there is no lower outlet)
Water: None

From 1957 to the mid-1960s this access road to Nordhoff Lookout was a well-maintained, graded dirt road and the favorite of local mountain bicyclists. Long-standing friction between the Forest Service and landowners, whose land the road crossed near Wheeler Hot Springs, led to abandonment of this route in the middle 1960s. But it still exists, and it is rideable from Nordhoff Peak down for about 4 miles and back up; however its condition is very bad near the lower end and there is no outlet down there. There are plans to plot property lines and lay out a bypass trail to connect with Highway 33, and this trail construction would be done by volunteers under the direction of the Forest Service.

Nordhoff Lookout Tower can still be seen, but the house on top is gone. Missing and loose planks make climbing the tower very dangerous, and in lightning storms the grounded metal tower should be avoided. At this time (1992) the best access to the tower is from Gridley Saddle to the east (see section B below).

From Nordhoff Peak to the Pratt Trail Junction you travel west along the ridge with an easy grade. Where the ridge rises, the road loops out to the south. Then when the main ridge drops more steeply the road cuts back to the north, descending more steeply to rejoin the main ridge. This is repeated again farther on past the Pratt Trail. The distance to the Pratt Trail is 0.6 mile with a 480' descent. The farther down you go, the rougher the road is, with the better areas right near the ridge top and in the saddles.

B. Gridley Saddle to Nordhoff Peak
Route/Trail: #5N08
Length: 1.0 mile
Level of Difficulty: Moderate; good road but steep climb
Elevation: 3,600' - 4,477'; 877' gain
Water: None
Campgrounds: None, although I have camped many times at the Lookout. Bring your own water. The view is great and the lights at night are memorable.

From Gridley Saddle you start this steep climb to the west up the ridge. First you ride on the north side a short distance around a switchback before crossing to the south, and you continue to climb with just a little break in the grade near the top. At the junction turn right and follow the road all the way around the peak, coming out right on top. A large flat area on the south side of the tower is a good place for an overnight stay.

Caution: Stay away from the tower and peak during rain or snowstorms due to lightning danger.

C. Gridley Saddle to Chief Peak Road
Route/Trail: #5N08
Length: 2.75 miles
Level of Difficulty: Moderate; steep climb first 1.25 miles; good road
Elevation: 3,600' - 5,000'; 1,400' gain
Water: None
Campgrounds: None; good overnight spot on the ridge at Howard Canyon Trail #22W26

When you leave Gridley Saddle and head east, you make a 900' climb in 1.25 miles. This steep ascent is all on the south side of the ridge and can be very hot at times. Almost at the top of the climb Howard Canyon Trail joins the road on the uphill north side marked by a wooden sign. Just past this junction the road crosses over Nordhoff Ridge to the north side. On your left is a flat area and a little farther east down a short steep hill is a saddle crossed by Howard Canyon Trail. This saddle or the flat above would be the most likely camp spot. Across the road to the east are roads to a nearby stock pond formed by a small dam. When there is water in the pond, mosquitoes could be a problem to campers and your presence could prevent wildlife from using the water.

From here on, the road stays on or very near the ridge top with a much less steep ascent, 500' of climbing in the next 1.5 miles. Along the ridge an occasional pole and some heavy wire are about all that remain of an old phone line from Nordhoff Lookout out along the ridge.

D. Chief Peak Road to Sisar Road

Route/Trail: Road #5N08
Length: 5.0 miles
Level of Difficulty: Easy graded road; a few short steep hills
Elevation: Start and end 5,000'; high point is 5,230'; low point is 4,750'
Water: None
Campgrounds: None; several places on the ridge would be okay

This is one of the best rides in the Ojai area. The views are exceptional, looking right down into the valley floor to the south and on the north looking across the Sespe at the Piedra Blanca formation and beyond to the cliffs of Reyes, Haddock, and Thorn Point peaks.

From the end of Chief Peak Road, head east on Nordhoff Ridge Road #5N08 and enjoy the nearly level travel after the steep climb you did to get there. Within a mile you will have descended and climbed a few short steep hills to the high point on this part of the road, only 230' higher than your start at Chief Peak Road. Some of these hills can be climbed with the momentum gained coming down the previous one. You come to the northwest corner of Chief Peak, where the road begins a long descent around the north and east sides of this triangular mountain. There are shaded places on the north side where snow lasts a surprisingly long time, and even on hot spring and fall days the ground remains frozen all day. On the south side of Chief Peak you will be at the low point of this part of the road at 4,750'. Here you head east again, and keeping to the north side of the ridge you climb 250' in 1 mile on a gradual grade to meet Sisar Road at a saddle. Then it's 8 miles all downhill to Highway 150 in Upper Ojai via Sisar Road.

E. Sisar Road to Topa Topa Bluff
Route/Trail: Road #5N08
Length: 4 miles
Level of Difficulty: Moderate; easy between Sisar Peak and Sisar Trail
Elevation: 5,000' - 5,500'
Water: None
Campgrounds: None, but there are several good overnight spots between Sisar Peak and Topa Topa Bluffs

This part of Road #5N08 connects to Lion Canyon Trail headed north down toward the Sespe and Sisar Trail going south to White Ledge Trail Camp and Sisar Road #4N15.

Starting from Sisar Road take Road #5N08, which circles around the north side of the first hill with little elevation gain before crossing a saddle to climb moderately to the south side of Sisar Peak. Here, after 1 mile and 300' of climbing, you will be at the top end of Horn Canyon Trail (not recommended for riding) and just south of Sisar Peak, easily recognized by all the repeater radio antennas on towers there. As you travel east close to the ridge top, the cliffs of Topa Topa Bluffs provide impressive scenery ahead. Enjoy some easy riding while descending slightly the next mile, and at the second saddle on the left make note of Lion Canyon Trail #22W06, marked by a sign. Just a half mile ahead on the right is the top of Sisar Canyon Trail #21W08. There are not many good reasons to make the climb to the Wilderness Boundary, which is 1.5 miles farther on the steep, rocky, north side of the bluffs. Bicycles are prohibited in wilderness areas.

Gridley Trail
Route/Trail: #5N11
Length: 6 miles
Level of Difficulty: Road moderate; trail expert
Elevation: 1,000' - 3,600'; 2,600' climb
Water: At Gridley Spring (former trail camp site) and Trail Spring
Parking: Along Gridley Road, off the pavement. If you're doing a loop trip, park on Grand Avenue, off the pavement. Do not block driveways.
Campgrounds: None (Gridley Spring Trail Camp was destroyed by flood)
Nearest Services: Ojai

Gridley Trail is the best single track on the Ojai front range. The grade is less than most rides and the lower part that was formerly a road is now a wide trail.

Almost all of it is rideable uphill. Gridley Canyon Road is not well maintained and has become mostly a trail. A long time ago it was possible to drive to Gridley Spring, which is why this trail has a road number.

Take Gridley Road north from Highway 150 past Grand Avenue through orange groves and up the foothills to near the end of Gridley Road, where a large trail sign indicates a trail easement through private property. This short trail, #22W05, connects to Gridley Canyon Road #5N11. Turn right here and pass through the avocado groves to a saddle. Take the left trail uphill, not the downhill road. After leaving the groves and entering Gridley Canyon, there are no other trails or roads until Gridley Saddle and Nordhoff Ridge Road #5N08.

Gridley Spring (3 miles) is in a very steep, narrow side canyon, and water runs down over bedrock and across the trail. A plastic pipe carries some of the water into a large water trough next to the trail for horses. The remains of an old redwood tank are on the hillside above the tank. (About a half mile down the trail another spring, which used to be just a seep, is running more very year and making the trail wet and muddy. Maple and sycamore trees grow there along with many other lush plants seldom seen on the mountainsides in this area.) Trail Spring is 1.5 miles above Gridley Spring in a gully on a very steep slope. The trail crosses below the spring; a short distance farther it switchbacks and passes above, where there is no trace of water.

During long summer days, we ride this trail after work. It's hot, but much of the trail is on the west side of Gridley Canyon and in shadow as the sun sets.

This area burned in the Wheeler Fire of July 1985, causing heat-fractured rocks to fall on the trail. In some areas of steep slopes, the trail was completely covered with rocks. The trail has been cleared and rerouted, but rocks continue to slide onto the trail. Short trail-clearing breaks are recommended here. The greatest hazard in this area is riding near steep drop-offs where a mishap can put you over the side, 100' or more down the hillside. Go slowly — or if you're not sure of your skill, get off and walk — and live to ride another day.

Sisar Canyon Road
Route/Trail: Road #4N15
Length: 8 miles
Level of Difficulty: Moderate
Elevation: 1,600' - 5,000'; 3,400' diff.
Water: Sisar Creek, White Ledge Spring, Wilsie Spring
Parking: Along Highway 150 next to Summit School
Campgrounds: White Ledge Trail Camp
Nearest Services: Upper Ojai; fire station 100 yards east of Sisar roadhead

Sisar Road has a fairly even, almost continuous grade and is usually in good condition. It's rideable all year, although in winter snow occurs at the upper elevations and in summer it can be very hot. During hot spells, start at dawn and ride uphill to stay in the shade on the southwest slopes.

From Highway 150, Sisar Road bears north just east of Summit School. Take all right forks until you reach the Forest Service locked gate. Beyond the locked gate there is one more fork, where you go left. (The right fork is a private road to a remote ranch–keep out. Trespassing here could cause loss of access to Sisar Road.)

The road switchbacks up Sisar Canyon to the junction of Sisar Canyon/Red Reef Trail #21W08. White Ledge Trail Camp, located a short distance up Trail #21W08, is a pleasant spot shaded by pungent bay trees. The spring here runs all year at considerable volume.

Past this junction with Trail #21W08, Sisar Canyon Road leaves the canyon and crosses a ridge out to the west of the canyon. Along the right side of the road at the 7 mile point, water is piped to a trough from Wilsie Spring just above the road. Horn Canyon Trail #22W08 crosses near the top of Sisar Canyon Road. It is a fairly good trail down to The Pines Trail Camp, which is located in a grove of pines. Spring water is piped to this camp from a nearby canyon. Due to the steep, rocky conditions, I don't recommend using Horn Canyon Trail below the camp.

Sisar Canyon Road ends on the top of the main ridge at Road #5N08, 1/2 mile above the Horn Canyon Trail junction.

Sisar Canyon/Red Reef Trail
Route/Trail: #21W08
Length: 3 miles
Level of Difficulty: Very difficult; steep, rutted, rocky and brushy. Downhill riding is only recommended above the camp.
Elevation: 5,250' - 3,300'; 1,950' descent
Water: White Ledge Spring
Campgrounds: White Ledge Trail Camp
Nearest Services: Upper Ojai via Sisar Road #4N15

In the mid-1960s roads were built along Nordhoff Ridge past Chief Peak and Topa Topa Bluff out to Hines Peak and down Sisar Canyon to Upper Ojai. These roads generally followed the route of the trails they replaced. In Sisar Canyon, though, the road takes a completely different route from 1 mile below White Ledge Trail Camp. This leaves a 3 mile section of the original Red Reef Trail intact in Sisar Canyon. (Before the roads were built, the Red Reef Trail went from Upper Ojai over the mountains and down Red Reef Canyon to the Sespe.)

This trail follows the creek up to White Ledge Trail Camp, keeping to the west side for 1 mile. Although the trail here is a little rough, it's not very steep, so it is okay to travel up to the camp. Springs here run all year and produce an amazing amount of water. The sites are in a grove of bay trees and the pleasant smell permeates the air. It's a nice camp, although level ground is limited.

Sometimes it is hard to find the trail leading uphill out of camp because the springs cause so much plant growth. Look above and slightly west of the upper camp site. Some short switchbacks here are also confusing, but the general trend of the trail is to follow up the ridge that starts right at the camp. It ascends with many switchbacks, sometimes through brush and in other places with ruts and stones left by storm runoff. Not all of this trail is rough, but some of it is steep, and with obstacles these parts cannot be ridden.

This trail is best ridden as a loop trip by riding up Sisar Road #4N15, then east on Road #5N08 to return down Sisar Canyon Trail back to Sisar Road and Upper Ojai. Total loop miles: 17.5.

Chief Peak Road
Route/Trail: #5N42.2
Length: 2.5 miles
Level of Difficulty: Very difficult, extremely steep in places
Elevation: 3,400' - 5,000'; 1,600' diff.
Water: None
Parking: Beside the lake below Rose Valley Falls Camp; you may not park in the campground unless you pay for a campsite
Campgrounds: Rose Valley Falls Camp, 9 sites, fee charged
Nearest Services: Ojai via Highway 33

Chief Peak Road was originally built as a fire road by the U.S. Navy Seabees Heavy Equipment Division, which was based at Rose Valley during the 1950s. They created the Rose Valley Lakes, improved Rose Valley Road, and left behind the base in Rose Valley that was later used as a County Jail Work Camp.

From Highway 33 at mile 25.84, take Rose Valley Road #6N31. When you see a small lake to the left, look for a road to the right to Rose Valley Falls and campground. Park at the upper lake. Ride into the campground and head right to a locked gate and road to the west. This road is very steep in places — so steep that even walking is difficult. Riding downhill, go slowly to avoid losing control. (The first time I saw this road I was on a downhill ride in 1959 on my Sears Roebuck J.C. Higgins coaster brake bike. By the time I got to the locked gate, my brakes were smoking, popping and sizzling.)

This road is the easiest way up to Nordhoff Ridge Fire Road #5N08. Best time up — 1 hour; average time — 1.5 hours.

Howard Canyon Trail

Route/Trail: #22W26
Length: 3 miles
Level of Difficulty: Difficult; narrow single track; steep places in the upper section
Elevation: 3,500' - 4,500', 1,000' diff.
Water: None
Parking: Turnout at trailhead 0.5 mile from Highway 33 on Rose Valley Road
Campgrounds: None
Nearest Services: Ojai via Highway 33

This trail was long ago abandoned because it traveled through a shooting area that was much abused. The shooting has since been banned, and local cyclists, Forest Service personnel, and other volunteers have restored this important trail. Although in many places the track is narrow and brush still needs cutting back, serious single-track riders enjoy the challenge of riding this trail uphill. Downhill is a lot of fun, and with more trail improvement it will be a blast.

One-half mile east of Highway 33 on the south side of Rose Valley Road, past some large pipe posts, is the present start of Howard Canyon Trail. It used to pass through the private property of Rancho Grande, 3/4 mile farther east. In the late 1960s a new road to Nordhoff Lookout from Rose Valley was started but never finished. It is this road, which crosses the Howard Canyon Trail, that is now the starting point in order to avoid the Rancho Grande property.

From Rose Valley Road you start south on Howard Canyon Trail by crossing a small drainage and keeping to the east of the trail, which was washed out by this stream. Head right and up steeply to the old road bed and follow it uphill, passing through a dense growth of Scotch Broom. You climb over a low ridge, pass through a road cut and descend to the west side, where you turn off to the left on the trail. It climbs with a gentle grade interspersed with very short, steep sections along the east side of the mountain and in and out of small canyons. The second canyon is larger and sometimes in spring it has water flowing. Just past here on the north side of the mountain the trail passes through a grove of oak trees — welcome shade on a hot day.

Turning again onto the east side of the mountain you can see down into Howard Canyon, where there are two small lakes. The trail continues on like this until you come to a slide area shored up by steel posts with board cribbing. Above here the trail is much steeper and more difficult for about 1/4 mile, and then you are almost at the top. At the ridge top the trail continues down and to the south to intersect the Nordhoff Ridge Road #5N08. You can also turn left on the ridge top, climb steeply a short way, and come out #5N08 where it crosses the ridge also. Just to the east is a dam and pond that usually has muddy water. Road #5N08 goes west to Gridley Saddle and east to Chief Peak Road #5N42.2.

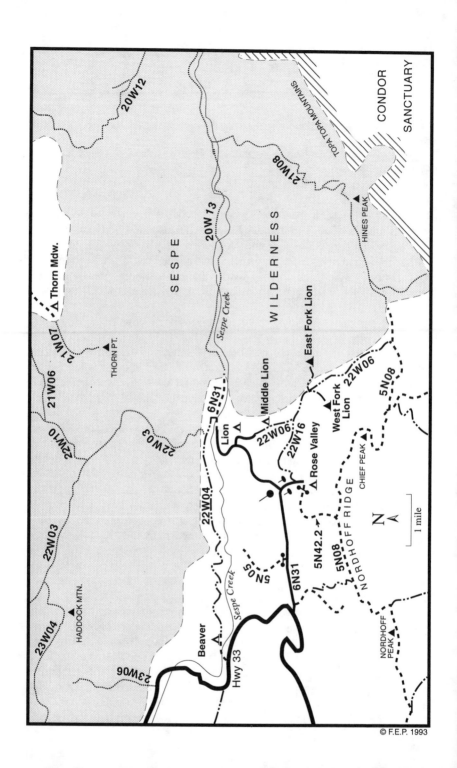

CONDOR SANCTUARY

TOPATOPA MOUNTAINS

20W12

21W08

HINES PEAK

20W 13

S E S P E

W I L D E R N E S S

Thorn Mdw.

21W07

21W06

THORN PT.

East Fork Lion

22W10

22W03

Sespe Creek

Middle Lion

6N31

West Fork Lion

22W06

5N08

Lion

22W06

22W16

Rose Valley

22W04

CHIEF PEAK

22W03

HADDOCK MTN.

N

1 mile

5N42.2

5N08

5N05

5N08

NORDHOFF RIDGE

6N31

23W04

Sespe Creek

Beaver

23W06

Hwy 33

NORDHOFF PEAK

© F.E.P. 1993

CHAPTER 4   SESPE CREEK
*Howard Creek Road, Rose Valley Falls Camp to Lion Canyon,
Lion Canyon Trail, Middle Sespe Trail, Sespe Creek Road*

To mountain bicyclists, the Sespe was a place that had the best this sport has to offer — both long and short rides, as well as fishing, swimming, and camping by the big pools on the river. And of course there are those fabled hot springs — so much boiling hot water it makes up a hot creek. The water cools flowing downstream, and you can find a pool with just the right temperature.

The Sespe is a place that seems timeless, and change is so gradual it's hard to see. The greatest changes came with management practices that allowed roads to be constructed along the river. Then with more people gaining access to gate keys, the barriers were opened to everyone in the early '60s. A nightmare of abandoned vehicles, drugs, and suspected murder was ended when the river floods of 1969 and 1972 washed out enough road to prevent 4WD traffic. Motor vehicles were prohibited, but bicycles were still allowed. Trails across Sespe Canyon made it possible to ride from the Lockwood Valley area to Ojai or Fillmore.

On June 19, 1992, the Los Padres Condor Range and River Protection Act was signed into law. This bill placed 219,700 acres of forest land along the Sespe Creek into wilderness status. All man-made structures — including stoves, tables, and corrals — are to be removed except for artifacts, foot trails, and registered historic buildings. Trail camps will be restored to a natural condition, and trails will be maintained at more primitive standards using only hand tools. Chain saws, some other motorized tools, and certain mechanical devices are prohibited. This includes bicycles.

Yes, bicycles are now prohibited from the Sespe. That's the law, and we have to live with it. Six years of lobbying while this bill was before Congress had no impact, and many miles of trails are now off limits to bicycles. (This guide book, revised with the cooperation and assistance of the Forest Service, describes only those trails that are outside the current wilderness boundary.) A few trails and roads are still open to cyclists in the Sespe upstream from the wilderness area, and some connect to adjoining areas.

Four drive-in campgrounds are located in this area. Beaver Camp is beside the Sespe Creek off Highway 33 at mile post 28.07. Rose Valley Falls, Middle Lion, and Lion Canyon campgrounds are all accessible by car over paved Rose Valley Road; turn off Highway 33 at mile post 28.84. Campfire restrictions may be in effect, so check ahead with the Forest Service.

Summer temperatures here are usually very hot with low humidity, and swimming in pools along the Sespe Creek is a popular summer pastime. Winter storms bring heavy rain and snow, causing road closures and raising streams so they become dangerous to cross.

Howard Creek Road

Route/Trail: #5N05
Length: 2 miles
Level of Difficulty: Easy; good beginner ride
Elevation: 3400' - 3300' (almost level)
Water: None
Parking: Off the pavement along Rose Valley Road near Howard Creek crossing
Campgrounds: None
Nearest Services: Ojai

This two-mile dirt road meanders north along Howard Creek from Rose Valley Road #6N31 to Sespe Creek. Turn left off Rose Valley Road 1.6 miles from Highway 33, just past the Howard Creek ford. A locked gate here restricts traffic to residents with cabins and homes at the road end. Do watch out for occasional traffic, and respect the rights of private property owners. This ride has little elevation change, and it's an easy down and back route novice riders should enjoy. Spring wildflowers have been good here, and a wild fire in 1991 will likely improve the showing.

Rose Valley Falls Camp to Lion Canyon

Route/Trail: #22W16
Length: 1.5 miles
Level of Difficulty: Moderate; some steep places
Elevation: 3400' - 3600'; 200' diff.
Water: Creek east of Rose Valley Falls; Lion Creek
Parking: Next to Upper Rose Valley Lake, just below Rose Valley Campground (do not park in campsites)
Campgrounds: Rose Valley Falls Camp
Nearest Services: Ojai

It is a 4-mile drive or ride from Highway 33 (milepost 25.84) on Rose Valley Road #6N31 to Rose Valley Falls Campground. From there, this short trail climbs over the ridge between the camp and Lion Canyon. The climb is steep in a few short stretches. From the parking area, go around the south side of the lake below the camp. The trail in this marshy area can be hard to find. From the south (Rose Valley Falls) side of the lake, the trail goes east and up a small creek that drains into the lake from the southeast. Soon, however, you come to a steep climb across a rocky slab and then into a brushy place before arriving atop a saddle. Here you can see down into Lion Canyon. Use care in descending because of ruts washed into the steep ridge below. Recent flooding washed out the trail where it crosses Lion Creek. You will have to make your way across to Lion Canyon trail on the east side. A very pleasant and scenic 5.5-mile loop ride can be taken by riding down Lion Canyon Trail to Middle Lion Camp and back on paved Rose Valley Road to Rose Valley Falls Camp.

Lion Canyon Trail is beside the Sespe Wilderness Boundary, and bicycles are not allowed on the trail to East Fork Lion Camp. The trail to the West Fork Camp is open, but as of this writing (fall 1992) it was in bad shape (see Lion Canyon Trail below).

Lion Canyon Trail
Route/Trail: #22W06
Length: 6 miles
Level of Difficulty: Moderate from Middle Lion Camp to trail fork to West Fork Camp (use special caution along steep drop-offs); very difficult above the fork
Elevation: 3200' to 5200'; 2000' diff.
Water: Lion Creek
Parking: Along Rose Valley Road before Lion Camp and on the right side of the camp road just before creek crossing (do not block campsites or roads)
Campgrounds: Middle Lion Camp at the trailhead
Nearest Services: Ojai

From Highway 33, drive 5 miles east on Rose Valley Road #6N31. Just before a large gate where the main road descends to the Sespe Creek, turn to the right and enter Lion Canyon, continuing to Middle Lion Camp. The road goes through the camp to the trailhead, crossing Lion Creek. This trail is popular with hikers and backpackers. *Ride with caution.* Enjoy the scenery but beware of steep drop-offs below some trail sections.

After climbing through a narrow section of canyon, the trail descends to a wider, more level area. At 1.5 miles you pass Trail #22W16 on the right, which connects to Rose Valley Falls Camp. Half a mile of nearly level trail in a very scenic canyon will bring you to a meadow where the trail splits three ways. The trail to West Fork Camp is on the right. A rough 0.4 mile will get you to the camp with three sites and seasonal water.

East Fork Camp and trail are in the Sespe Wilderness and are closed to bicycles. (It is one-half mile to the camp.)

Straight ahead the main trail climbs the central ridge. From here it's a serious climb with rock sections and shale slides. (A trail crew cleared brush in 1991.) No water is available on the trail above the forks at the meadow. Four miles above the junction, the trail ends at road #5N08 on the ridge above. Retrace your route or ride west to connect with roads or trails to Upper Ojai, Ojai, or Rose Valley.

Middle Sespe Trail
Route/Trail: #22W04
Length: 6 miles
Level of Difficulty: Very difficult (as of fall 1992) due to brush and erosion
Elevation: 3300' - 3800' - 3000'
Water: Rock Creek and Sespe Creek
Parking: At Beaver Camp just off Highway 33 (mile 28.07) and at Lion Camp on Sespe Creek (check parking regulations)
Campgrounds: Beaver Camp, Lion Cam
Nearest Services: Ojai

The Sespe Wilderness boundary runs right along the north side of this trail, meaning it's legal to ride, but trail conditions have deteriorated badly the last few years. The eastern part from Rock Creek to Piedra Blanca Trail has brushed in and needs clearing. The trail west of Rock Creek burned in a fire that got away from Lion Camp in the fall of 1991. Heavy winter rains that followed in 1992 washed out large parts of the trail where it passes over an 800-foot hill just west of Rock Creek. Trail crews are scheduled to rework this whole trail soon. When that happens, the route along the north bank of the Sespe can be part of a good loop by riding back on Rose Valley Road and Highway 33. In summer, bring a bathing suit for a dip in Sespe Creek. Check updated trail conditions at the Ojai District Ranger Office.

From Beaver Camp you must cross Sespe Creek to the east side. Stream flooding washes out the trail every winter, so it is sometimes hard to find. It heads southeast a little and then east on benches above the north side of the river. The first mile continues to meander with no great elevation change until suddenly you are faced with a steep climb on almost bare slopes up switchbacks through the burn and over an 800-foot hill to Rock Creek. (This is across the Sespe from Howard Creek). From Rock Creek to Lion Camp you ride in and out of little side canyons rising and dropping a little on the way. Near Lion Camp the trail to Piedra Blanca branches north (in wilderness and off limits to bicycles). Keep right and descend to Sespe Road #6N31. Here you can see across the river to Lion Camp and the end of the trail (see *Parking*). A 15-mile loop is possible by riding back on the paved road.

Sespe Creek Road
Route/Trail: #6N31
Length: 1.25 miles
Level of Difficulty: Easy; almost no hills; very muddy when wet
Elevation: 3000' - 2950'
Water: Piedra Blanca Creek; sometimes Trout Creek
Parking: Lions Camp day use parking area
Campgrounds: Lions Camp drive-in campground
Nearest Services: Ojai

The wilderness boundary takes a jog around two parcels of private property that lie along the river to just below Trout Creek. The boundary crosses the old road at a gate where you start to climb away from the Sespe Creek. You may ride bicycles from Lions Camp to this gate, but no farther.

After crossing the Sespe Creek at Lions Camp heading northeast, you will be at the junction of Piedra Blanca Trail, Middle Sespe Trail and Sespe Road #6N31. Heading east on the road you cross Piedra Blanca Creek after 0.6 mile and Trout Creek at 1.1 miles. A fast down and back takes about 30 minutes, so take your time to savor the scenery and watch out for people doing the same on foot. This is just a sample of what the next 15 miles are like. Come back with your hiking boots or trail running shoes and get into the wilderness for a while.

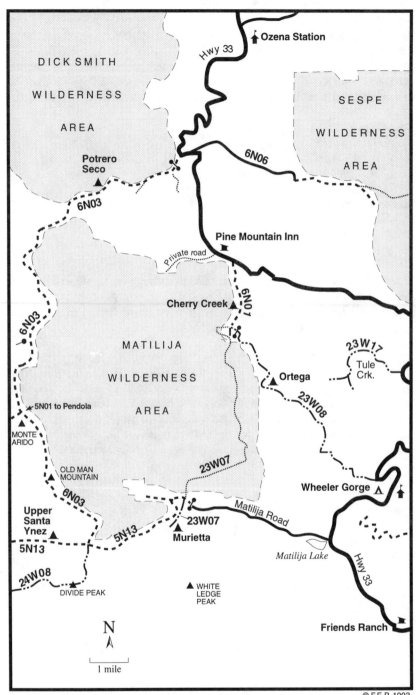

Ozena Station

Hwy 33

DICK SMITH
WILDERNESS
AREA

6N06

SESPE
WILDERNESS
AREA

Potrero
Seco

6N03

Pine Mountain Inn

Private road

6N01

Cherry Creek

23W17

Tule
Crk.

6N03

MATILIJA
WILDERNESS
AREA

Ortega

23W08

5N01 to Pendola

MONTE
ARIDO

OLD MAN
MOUNTAIN

23W07

Wheeler Gorge

6N03

Upper
Santa
Ynez

5N13

23W07

Matilija Road

Murietta

Matilija Lake

Hwy 33

5N13

24W08

DIVIDE PEAK

WHITE
LEDGE
PEAK

Friends Ranch

N

1 mile

© F.E.P. 1993

CHAPTER 5   MATILIJA
Murietta Road, Bald Hills Road, Cherry Canyon Road, Ortega Trail, Monte Arido Road, Tule Creek Trail

The same bill that created the Sespe Wilderness also included the 29,600-acre Matilija Wilderness. However, Upper North Fork Matilija Trail is the only trail here closed to bicycles because of wilderness status. And, although it is a popular hiking trail, the Wheeler Fire of 1985 and 6 years of drought killed many of the alders along the stream, which are rotting at the base and falling across the trail.

Trails and roads bordering the Matilija Wilderness are open to bicycles and are described here. This area of long, narrow, twisting canyons is bordered on the east by Highway 33 and on the west by a long ridge along the Santa Barbara County line. Before Highway 33 was extended north of Wheelers, the Matilija Upper North Fork-Cherry Creek Trail was the main access to the Upper Sespe. Fishermen, hunters, and cattle ranchers traveled this way, packing in supplies and even driving cattle on this trail. John Dent and his family, long time Ventura County ranchers, traveled this way from their Ventura ranch to their Pine Mountain ranch. The Dent family home, formerly on North Ventura Avenue, was sold and moved by its new owner to the end of the paved road up Matilija Canyon. I can't imagine what John Dent would say if he could see where his house ended up.

Ridge-top trails and roads, very steep in some places, provide views of wilderness both close by and to the far horizons. Streams have water all year and some have native trout. This area receives the most rainfall in the county and streams become impassable at flood stage, so take care while riding during the rainy season. The abrupt turns of the canyons offer remote solitude, and make self-reliance a must for riding here.

Trail camps are located at Murietta Canyon, Cherry Canyon, and Ortega Ridge. The Ortega Ridge Trail was built by and is maintained by 4WD clubs. All levels of riding experience are possible here; the more remote areas require the most expertise and care.

Murietta Road
Route/Trail: #5N13
Length: 5 miles
Level of Difficulty: Moderate. Easy approach and lower canyon; steep and rougher the last mile. Check downhill speed.
Elevation: 1600' - 3400'; 1800' diff.
Water: At springs along the roadside
Parking: Parking area at the locked gate end of Matilija Road
Campgrounds: Murietta Trail Camp
Nearest Services: Ojai

This road travels 5 miles on the north side of Murietta Canyon from Matilija Creek to Murietta Divide. You can get to the trailhead by taking Lake Matilija County Road east from Highway 33 (milepost 16.28), 5 miles north of Ojai. Go past Lake Matilija and continue to a parking area at the locked Forest Service gate. Ride on the Forest Service easement past a relocated old house and cross Matilija Creek twice on the dirt road. You'll pass the wilderness trail to Upper North Fork Matilija #23W07 on the right. Next, on the left, Trail #24W07 is a pleasant, short half-mile to Murietta Trail Camp alongside the oak-shaded creek. A volunteer trail project has connected #24W07 from Murietta Camp to the main Murietta Road, with additional improvements planned for the future.

Continue up Matilija Canyon to the west until Road #5N13 turns left at a house and gate. Here, one mile past the paved road, you leave Matilija Canyon and enter Murietta Canyon. When water flow at the crossings is low, this first mile is very easy and a worthwhile ride in itself. By looking up to the southwest, you can see the road ahead climbing around a ridge into Murietta Canyon.

As you begin riding up into Murietta Canyon, the road switches back to the east first, with a splendid view of the canyons below. Turning west again into Murietta Canyon, the grade remains very rideable. Look into the canyon at the 1.8 mile point and you can see Murietta Trail Camp next to the stream in a grove of oak trees. Continue climbing on a well-graded road and then enjoy a break with a slight descent to where, at 2.8 miles, the road crosses a small stream with abundant water. Past this stream the climb keeps increasing, getting noticeably steeper and rougher around 3.7 miles. A notable feature of this canyon are large ferns growing at the many springs near the roadside. They are very dense at 4.2 miles by a spring that is piped under the road to a water trough on the south side. Incredibly the road gets even steeper, challenging many riders' determination to ride all the way to the top (if they have made it this far). Riding down this very steep and rocky upper canyon road requires good braking control at all times.

From Murietta Divide the road continues west as Juncal Canyon Road #5N13, and it also connects to Monte Arido Road #6N03 (north) and Divide Peak Trail #24W08 (south). From Murietta Divide, if you continue on Road #5N13 down Juncal Canyon about 1 mile, you'll find Santa Ynez Trail Camp next to a year-round running stream. This trail camp with shady oak trees and water is the only camp near the divide.

Bald Hills Road

Route/Trail: No number
Length: 0.8 mile
Level of Difficulty: Easy
Elevation: 1750' - 1950'; 2800' diff.
Water: None
Parking: Parking area at the end of Matilija Road near a locked gate
Campgrounds: Murietta Trail Camp
Nearest Services: Ojai

Follow the same directions as Murietta Road (above): paved Matilija Canyon Road to locked gate parking area; easy ride one mile west on graded dirt road with two stream crossings. Bald Hills Road continues west where Murietta Road doubles back to the east and up the mountainside. To follow the Bald Hills Road west, pass through a gate at this junction. A home with many outbuildings is along the roadside and from the gate to the wilderness boundary, 0.8 mile ahead, this road is on private property. Stay on the main road, keeping off driveways and side roads.

When you have traveled almost to the second place of habitation, the road splits. The right fork is a driveway, so keep to the left. Soon, just east of Old Man Canyon, this double track becomes a trail and enters the wilderness, where it is no longer legal to ride.

While traveling on this road, look to the northwest at the slopes between Old Man Canyon and Westfall Canyon. Bushes and grasses there are always very short over a large area, hence the name Bald Hills. A very long time ago the trail climbed up through these hills, crossed Westfall Canyon and climbed very steeply to join the ridge trail north of Monte Arido. The Bald Hills Trail may be reopened someday, but not to bicycles because it is all in the wilderness.

Cherry Canyon Road
Route/Trail: #6N01
Length: 2.5 miles
Level of Difficulty: Easy to moderate
Elevation: 4100' - 5000', 900' diff.
Water: Infrequent; carry your own supplies
Parking: Along Highway 33 at turnouts near mile post 38.22
Campgrounds: Cherry Creek Trail Camp
Nearest Services: Ojai

Special caution: Target shooters have been using the lower canyon on both sides of the road.

Cherry Canyon Road is a good road with a moderate grade except for a short, steep hill near the top. The road was used during construction of a gas pipeline that crosses Sespe Creek and goes up the ridge east of Cherry Creek. It is now open to OHV (Off-Highway Vehicle) traffic, so watch and listen for 4WDs and motorcycles. This route is rideable except during snow or high water at Sespe crossing. One trail camp, although not in good repair, is located 2/3 of the way up on the right. (To reach the camp, cross the creek and climb up to the tables and fire pits.)

At the top of Ortega Saddle, Cherry Canyon Road connects with Ortega OHV Road and Trail #23W08 to the east (see ride below). The Matilija Wilderness boundary is all along the west side (on your right headed uphill) of Cherry Canyon Road. The boundary curves to the east at the saddle, cutting across Trail #22W07 where it descends into Upper North Fork Matilija Canyon, which is closed to bicycles.

Ortega Trail

Route/Trail: #23W08
Length: 8 miles one way
Level of Difficulty: Difficult; steep most parts with many rocks on the trail
Elevation: 5000' to 2250'; 2750' diff.
Water: None
Parking: Highway 33. For Cherry Canyon roadhead park at mile 38.22; for lower trailhead park at mile 20.71.
Campgrounds: Ortega Trail Camp
Nearest Services: Ojai

From the top down on this ride you have 3 miles of rough 4WD road and 5 miles of rocky motorcycle trail. You stay on ridges almost all the way with no real stream crossings. This is a historic trail used to get to the upper Sespe before the paved highway was built past Wheelers. It was an alternate, usable when high water or downed trees blocked Upper North Fork Matilija Canyon trail. Sheep were sometimes grazed in the area of the old Ortega Camp. The drainage from around the old camp crosses the trail 1/2 mile below the camp, passing under very large boulders and out of sight of anyone on the trail. A story of the sheep herder watering his animals by lowering a bucket down to the water between the boulders caught my interest. Sure enough, only about 30 feet upstream from the trail are some very deep openings between the boulders with water there in the early summer. If you were to fall or somehow get stuck in one of these deep remote holes, you might not be found for a long time. Another historical note: about a mile up from the lower trailhead is a carved rock next to the trail on the south (uphill) side. An outline of a church and J. B. KING JAN 30 1908 is carved very neatly, except for the N in KING, which is done backward.

To ride Ortega Trail from the top of Cherry Creek Road #6N01, take Road #23W08 left (east) along the ridge and then down on the south side of Ortega Hill. It starts as a 4WD road and soon becomes a very steep downhill run. At the bottom, the trail climbs a wash and comes out on the ridge between Tule Canyon and Matilija North Fork Canyon. On this ridge the 4WD road ends and the route continues as trail. 4WD clubs have created the present Ortega Trail Camp, and there's no water here. Old maps and a couple of stoves show where the original Ortega Camp was located — 2.75 miles farther down the trail. The 4WD roads in this area are actually Caterpillar tractor trails left from the construction of the gas pipeline that stretches from Coalinga to the coast and follows the ridge nearby. The pipeline was built in the late '50s, and scars created by its construction are still visible. At its lower end, this trail switchbacks down to Highway 33 (mile 20.71) at a 180° turn of the highway just above the

Holiday Group Camp.

If you feel tough enough, do this as a loop. Park near Highway 33's milepost 20.71, ride up the highway to Cherry Canyon Road #6N01 (milepost 38.22), and take Cherry Canyon Road to Ortega Trail. Return to the start via Ortega Trail as described above. You could also have someone drop you off or use two cars for a shuttle. Due to the steep grade, riding up this trail from Highway 33 is not recommended.

Monte Arido Road

Route/Trail: #6N03
Length: 20 miles
Level of Difficulty: Moderate to Potrero Seco; more difficult to Monte Arido; very difficult near Old Man Mountain; many steep hills; long distance
Elevation: 5080' - 6000' - 3400'
Water: None
Parking: Highway 33 at Pine Mountain Summit Pass (milepost 42.7)
Campgrounds: Potrero Seco Trail Camp (4WD access with permit)
Nearest Services: Ojai

Special considerations: Winter storms bring heavy snow, and the adobe mud is bad during spring thaw. Riding into the area on frozen roads in the morning can leave you stuck with a noon thaw miles from the highway.

This ridge-top road provides exceptional views of wilderness landscapes with few man-made alterations. Most of those are historic ranches at the northern end of the road, between Highway 33 and Potrero Seco. In this area, the road runs near the border of the Dick Smith Wilderness, and from many high points you can look out over most of the wilderness to the northwest. The southern 15 miles of the ride takes you along the border of the Matilija Wilderness to the east, with excellent views down into remote, steep, narrow canyons. Following the ridge, the road climbs and drops many times.

Excellent day rides can be enjoyed by parking at the upper roadhead and traveling into Potrero Seco, returning the way you came in. Three miles one way takes less than an hour with only a net descent of 150 feet. A more strenuous effort will take you farther out to the Three Sisters Rocks, 7 miles and 2 hours one way. (These times include a lot of sightseeing. Fast riders can do it in half the time.) Bring a map, compass, and binoculars to locate distant landmarks; by remembering them you will be able to tell where you are. Riding past the Three Sisters puts you farther into the mountains on a ridge that gets tougher the farther you go. Somewhere about the 10-mile mark you need to decide to go back or continue past the point where turning back is not a good option.

Starting from Pine Mountain Summit Pass, head west past the locked gate. Watch out for occasional motor vehicle traffic operated here under special permit from the Forest Service. Right away you have a steep descent and climb to a saddle at 0.3 mile, where a good road branches to the south, climbing slightly for 0.2 mile to a locked gate posted "No Trespassing." Continuing west on Road #6N03 from the saddle, you climb a little more easily to the ridge. Riding close to the ridge top you can see a deep canyon to the south; past that you cross a cattle guard (0.8 mile). A spur road branches southwest here to the Dent Ranch, and the main road passes between pine trees to the west. There is more easy riding and you start passing the first large grass slopes; then at the top of a grade (1.6 miles) you can see down across the Potrero Seco and the headwaters of the Sespe. Two ranches are situated alongside the creek among the cottonwood trees. The descent to the ranches is twofold, with the two downhill runs separated by a slight climb over a saddle. At you approach the ranches keep right, cross a cattle guard (2.25 miles), and climb toward the west across a gently sloping field.

Just before a large green tank, take a road on the right 100 yards to Potrero Seco Trail Camp, 3 miles from the start. The camp is set in a hollow with hills on three sides, open to the east. There are three tables and fireplaces shaded by oak and pine trees, but no water. Just northeast is the abandoned site of the old Potrero Seco Guard Station.

Going farther on Monte Arido Road #6N03, you first climb moderately for a mile, and then on the right pass the Loma Victor Road #7N05 that descends on a ridge along the Dick Smith Wilderness boundary to Mono Creek and Don Victor Valley. Past this junction you climb a little more and make a steep descent to a saddle, where there is a short side road south to a dam and pond. On this saddle at 6.2 miles the Three Sisters Rocks can be seen ahead. A short steep climb gets you to these surprisingly large, isolated sandstone boulders at 6.8 miles. Shade and wind protection is available here, making it a good rest stop. The Hildreth Jeepway, Road #6N17, starts here past a locked gate on the north side of the rocks and can be seen along the ridge out to Hildreth Peak to the west. From Potrero Seco to these rocks, the road has been gradually turning to the south and now the rest of the way is generally south.

A gate at 7.0 miles is the start of a very fast section, slightly downhill on good graded road. The climb ahead is typical with some short, steep, walk-and-push hills mixed with rideable areas — you go over a peak, down a steep hill, and repeat it again. Another gate (locked) at 12.2 miles is next to a dam and pond on the west side of the road. Climb again to the northwest side of Monte Arido and at 12.45 miles pass the Pendola Jeepway, Road #5N01, which heads down into an open saucer-shaped canyon before descending the ridge to Pendola Station at Agua Caliente Canyon. (Experienced mountain bicyclists seeking a tough, challenging ride can start at Juncal Camp and ride up past Murietta Divide, making the steep climb to Monte Arido and returning by the Pendola Jeepway.)

Monte Arido, 13.2 miles along and 6003' elevation, is the highest point on Road #6N03. You can make the short walk to the summit, just west and a little above the road. The next 1.5 miles has the steepest descent, so use your brakes to keep control and lower your bicycle seat if possible. From another saddle on the north side of Old Man Mountain, the road climbs around on the west slopes of this double peak, giving you a good view looking down to Juncal Dam and Jameson Lake. When I am really tired of climbing, there are the two similar uphills where they shouldn't be on the south side of Old Man Mountain. Finally you lose altitude, steeply, with many switchbacks across a barren-looking landscape.

That scene changes suddenly while you make a short climb past pine trees growing among large sandstone boulders. There is more steep descending across a boulder garden until at 19 miles a road to your right leads to a small lake, too improbable to be overlooked. One more mile and at 20 miles even you are at Murietta Divide, which is pleasantly level after so much downhill. Going back up this mountain on the south side on a hot sunny day would be a grueling task. If you planned ahead, ride down Murietta and Matilija canyons to your second vehicle, parked along Highway 33 at Matilija Lake Road.

Tule Creek Trail
Route/Trail: #23W17
Length: 1.5 miles
Level of Difficulty: Moderate; the difficulty here is due to trail conditions (rocks and bushes)
Elevation: 3450' - 3650'; 200' diff.
Water: Where water is flowing in the creek bed
Parking: At the turnout along Highway 33 (mile 29.65) across from the trail
Campgrounds: Beaver Camp, located just off Highway 33 at milepost 28.07
Nearest Services: Ojai

Tule Creek is a fascinating area. Brush, trees, wildflowers, grasses, and, of course, tules grow here. The canyon twists and turns and keeps revealing open areas that always appear to end, only to turn and reveal more canyon again. Tule Creek is a wonder in summer because it runs underground for short distances where the stream bed is dry, only to reappear and run noisily for a ways, repeating this same pattern many times. Where it does run all year you can find native trout confined to short sections of stream.

The trail starts at the southwest side of Tule Creek Bridge (Highway 33 mile marker 29.65), then crosses Tule Creek to the north side and stays north of Tule Creek for another mile. Just before a clump of trees, the trail abruptly crosses Tule Creek and continues on the south side, becoming fainter all the time. Take it slow and easy to avoid erosion and rocks hidden in vegetation that covers this short trail.

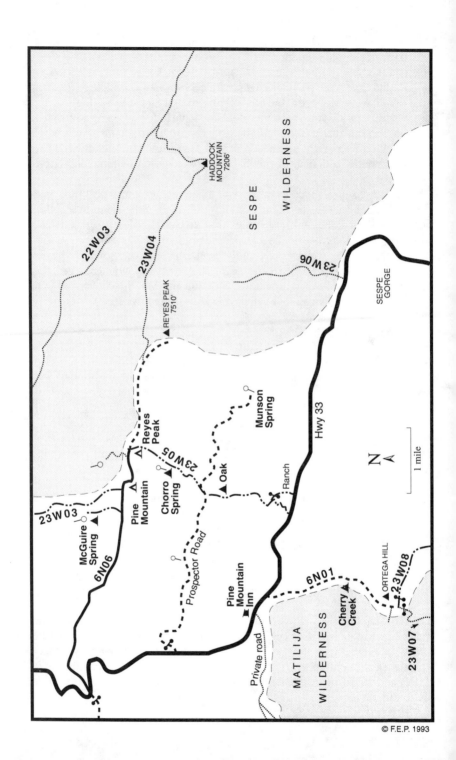

CHAPTER 6   PINE MOUNTAIN
Pine Mountain Road, Chorro Grande Trail, Prospector Road

Pine Mountain is a high ridge running east 14 miles from Pine Mountain Summit Pass (5,080') on Highway 33. The north and south slopes are very steep with short, nearly parallel canyons running along the south side. Reyes Peak (7,510') and Haddock Mountain (7,206') are the highest points, and both are within the new Sespe Wilderness. Looking north from Ventura, the highest, most distant peak seen is Pine Mountain, 30 miles away. Winter snow there is visible from Ventura, but the many large pines above 6,000 feet are not readily apparent from a great distance.

At Pine Mountain Summit, Highway 33 (mile 42.7), drive east on the paved ridge road for great car-camping areas that give the mountain cyclist access to some of the most scenic rides around. You'll find campsites among the tall pines and near large sandstone outcroppings. The daytime views both north and south are tremendous, and clear nights offer outstanding views of city lights at the beach and masses of stars in the sky. *Caution:* Bring all your own water. None is available on the ridge top.

The pavement ends just past the last developed campsite near the Chorro Grande Trail junction. Mountain biking on the unpaved ridge road to Reyes Peak is fairly easy. Chorro Grande Trail descends steeply to the south past two trail camps — the upper one next to a spring — and ends at Highway 33. Prospector Road, an 8-mile dirt road, traverses the south slopes, crossing Chorro Grande Trail.

Pine Mountain Road
Route/Trail: #6N06
Mileage: 6 miles paved one-lane road, then 1.5 miles of dirt road
Level of Difficulty: Easy, but with a high altitude 2,020' climb on paved road
Elevation: 5,080' - 7,100'; 2,020' diff.
Water: None
Parking: At turnout off Highway 33 at mile 42.7, or at campground parking areas and roadside parking on Pine Mountain Road
Campgrounds: Several camps along the paved road, but no developed sites on the dirt portion out to Reyes Peak
Nearest Services: Cafe at Pine Mountain Inn, food and drink; phone at the USFS Ozena Station to the north and Wheeler Gorge Station to the south

You can start riding Pine Mountain Road #6N06 from the junction with Highway 33 or from any of the camps along the way. The height of this mountain provides extensive views of the backcountry. The dirt section of Road #6N06 is graded, in good repair, and fairly level. Although open to motor vehicles, there's not much traffic here. This road connects to Chorro Grande

Trail #23W05 (see below). Be sure to bring plenty of water; there is none available on the mountain top and it is 1 mile down to Raspberry Spring on the north and 0.8 mile down to Chorro Spring on the south.

At the end of the dirt section of the road at the wilderness boundary is Reyes Peak Trail #23W04, which is closed to bicycles.

Chorro Grande Trail
Route/Trail: #23W05
Mileage: 5.4 miles
Level of Difficulty: Very difficult above Prospector Road, moderate below
Elevation: 4,050' - 7,100'; 3,050' diff.
Water: Chorro Spring or Chorro Grande Creek (near Oak Trail Camp)
Parking: At the upper (northern) end, park near the pavement-dirt junction, just past the last campsite on Road #6N06. Park off to the side out of traffic. At the lower (southern) end, use the turnout off Highway 33 at mile 36.6.
Campgrounds: Car campsites along Road #6N06; Chorro Spring and Oak trail camps on #23W05
Nearest Services: Cafe at Pine Mountain Inn, food and drink; phone at the USFS Ozena Station to the north and Wheeler Gorge Station to the south

This trail passes through three zones with sudden, dramatic terrain and vegetation changes. From the top at 7,100 feet you ride down 600 feet in 1 mile, passing through a scattered pine and fir forest where most of the yearly precipitation is snowfall. Melting snow causes very little erosion here. The middle 2 miles drop steeply (1,000 feet) on a ridge through low-growing chaparral and areas with severe erosion. These two upper zones are too steep to ride up, so start from Road #6N06.

If you want to just ride the lowest zone — a canyon and stream-side environment — park at miles 36.6 along Highway 33. Here are 2 miles of trail with only a 400 foot net gain, large sandstone formations to explore, wildflower meadows, and Oak Trail Camp under spreading shade trees.

Strong riders can make a scenic and challenging loop using this trail. Get an early start from the lower trailhead, mile 36.6, and ride up Highway 33 to the summit pass at mile 42.7. Turn right and go 6 miles up Pine Mountain Road #6N06 to Chorro Grande Trail. Take a right and ride this single track 5.4 miles back down to the starting point for a 17.5 mile loop.

To ride the length of Chorro Grande Trail from Pine Mountain Road, start where the pavement ends at a gate (seasonal closure during wet weather). Here a sign directs you to Chorro Grande Trail, which appears to plunge down the south side of the mountain. By looking carefully you should be able to see the switchbacks that others have cut across. Past these short switchbacks the trail traverses east along the slopes through mixed forest. At 0.45 mile you pass through an open, flattish area before descending more steep rocky sections. Chorro Camp and spring are at 0.8 mile at an excellent location in a little hollow filled with large trees. The spring is under a huge boulder and forms a pool in a small cave before running down the canyon. One campsite is right next to the spring and another is about 75 feet uphill next to a 4-foot diameter fir tree. A third, less-used site is located just east of the lower trail sign.

Riding out of this little canyon, you suddenly leave the tall trees behind and enter low chaparral on steep slopes. Here at 1 mile you can view the Sespe below and clear to its headwaters at the Potrero Seco grassland to the west. For the next 2 miles the trail descends a ridge into Chorro Grande Canyon. Slow travel is required along rocky sections and areas of sharp switchbacks. Wildflowers are abundant all along this ridge and in the canyon below. At 2.9 miles the trail widens when it joins an old cat road by the stream. Soon at 3.0 miles you cross Prospector Road. Be sure to cross the stream here in late spring to see a meadow filled with Matilija poppies—five inches across—blooming white and yellow.

Chorro Grande Trail is much easier to ride below Prospector Road. The catway roads here are part of an extensive mineral prospect across the south side of Pine Mountain. Looking east near mile 3.3, a large open cut with tailings is evident. At the bottom of a short, steep, rocky hill at 3.6 miles is a flat with Oak Camp beside the trail. It has three sites well apart from each other under shady oak trees. The creek beside this camp dries out sometimes, but water can generally be found upstream within a half mile. After traveling over some low hills on your way down the canyon, you will come to a trail junction. The trail you need turns right abruptly and can be missed. (The trail straight ahead passes onto private land and is used by horse riders from the pack station below.) Continuing down the right fork on Chorro Grande Trail, a very large sandstone formation is encountered at 4.4 miles. The trail then crosses two creeks and a small wash, dropping and climbing steeply at each until at 4.75 miles a high point is reached. Then it's downhill on a good single track to the highway at 5.4 miles.

Prospector Road
Route/Trail: No number
Mileage: 4.6 miles to Chorro Grande Trail; 8 miles total
Level of Difficulty: Moderate
Elevation: 4,500' - 5,200'; many ups and down
Water: Goodwin Creek, Chorro Grande Creek, Burro Creeks, Munson Spring
Parking: Highway 33 turnouts at mile 40.5, at Chorro Grande Trailhead (mile 36.6), or at Pine Mountain Inn (mile 38.9)
Campgrounds: Oak Trail Camp, 0.5 mile down Chorro Grande Trail. Possible car-camping at Pine Mountain Inn; fee required.
Nearest Services: Cafe at Pine Mountain Inn, food and drink; phone at the USFS Ozena Station to the north and Wheeler Gorge Station to the south

This hidden road winds its way east for 8 miles, roughly parallel to and about a mile north of Highway 33. It dips in and out of canyons that drain the south side of Pine Mountain ridge. The first 2 miles, shown on topo and Forest Service maps, are very old. The other 6 miles, along with many spur roads, were built by prospectors looking for gypsum deposits here in the late 1960s. They staked mineral claims and still maintain the road but do not have title to the land, which is open for recreation. The end of the original 2.1-mile road passes through private property for about 3/4 mile. Please respect this property, which is currently not posted.

I especially like this road because the hills are short with only a minor elevation change of 600 feet. The varied terrain keeps my interest with new views and conditions every mile. This is a ride I want to share with my friends as a day ride and also for overnight trips. A special hazard here is a tenacious glue-like adobe soil that, if wet from rain or snow melt, sticks to everything it touches.

For a short ride up and back, park in the Highway 33 turnout just up the hill from the roadhead at the 40.5 milepost, or park by Pine Mountain Inn and ride up the highway 1.6 miles to the roadhead.

A longer loop ride is best done by parking at Pine Mountain Inn, riding up the highway, doing Prospector Road to Chorro Grande Trail, going down the trail to Highway 33, and riding the highway back to the start at Pine Mountain Inn. This totals 10.5 miles with 3.9 miles on the highway and 2 miles downhill on single-track trail. (If you park at Pine Mountain Inn, let them know where you are going and be sure not to block their drive.)

The highway climbs steadily to the northwest from the Inn through a pine-forested canyon, which narrows noticeably near Prospector Road, 1.6 miles from the Inn at milepost 40.5. Prospector Road is on the right past a locked gate at the highway. Ride down and cross Adobe Creek, then turn right and enter a narrow canyon. Some short steep climbs and creek crossings at 0.5 and 0.7 mile take you past the narrow part of the canyon where many varieties of trees grow (oak, pine, fir, willow, bay, and others).

At 0.8 mile the canyon opens up and the road turns to the east, switchbacking and climbing out of the canyon. This hill starts out steep but gets easier near the top, where, at 1.3 miles, you have a good view of the grassy hillsides ahead. A short spur road to the right ends at a guzzler. This is a fiberglass water catcher and cistern to provide water for wildlife.

Next you have some level riding before a sharp right turn and a steady climb across a grassy hill. For the next 3/4 mile the road crosses private property. Keep to the main route and avoid the spur roads in this area. When you reach the upper end of the grassland — at 2.1 miles with a spur road to the left and a large pine on the right — you are on the high point of this road at 5,200 feet.

From here, Prospector Road is rougher and drops steeply into a small canyon, but it comes out the other side with an easy grade. There is an open gate just before you get to another ridge at 2.5 miles, where a deeper canyon can be seen ahead. This is the west fork of Godwin Canyon, and for the next 2 miles you get to know the other two forks by descending into and climbing out of them. The climbs are not as bad as they look. The scenery is wild and the ridges between the canyons offer good views and possible camping or lunch opportunities.

Soon, at 4.4 miles, you are looking down into Chorro Grande Canyon with the road below crossing a meadow of Matilija poppies. You can also see Chorro Grande Trail descending with switchbacks and then crossing Prospector Road just east of the creek. There is usually water in the creeks. There at 4.6 miles you can head down Chorro Grande Trail 2 miles to Highway 33 (see previous ride) and back north 2.3 miles to Pine Mountain Inn. Or you can choose to go on to Munson Canyon and return, 3.4 miles one way by a rougher, steeper road.

To continue to Munson Canyon, cross Chorro Canyon Trail on Prospector Road, which curves north with a steep climb for 0.3 mile. On top it is suddenly flat with oak trees in level clearings in the brush. A spur road runs out the ridge to the south and ends on a small peak. Cross the flat, go into a dip and short climb to a high point, and you can look into the east branch of Chorro Grande Canyon. It's a steep, rocky descent to the bottom at 1.1 miles from Chorro Grande Trail. You have a substantial climb out the other side of this canyon, starting with an easy grade and ending with 100 yards of walking to the top at 1.6 miles. Here, in a saddle at 5,000 feet, a spur road climbs to the south and then descends and climbs on a ridge a quarter mile away.

Next Prospector Road winds down into Burro Canyon and crosses the creek at 2.2 miles. Then it heads down the canyon with an easy grade on the east side of the creek where, at 2.4 miles, there is a sweeping 180° turn to the left. You end up heading north again and climbing steeply back up to another saddle. Here at 2.8 miles you finally see into Munson Canyon. First you have a short, steep descent, then some level road until on the west side of the canyon the road gives out and it is a very steep descent to the canyon bottom. Across the canyon, just up from the bottom, is Munson Spring. It gushes out of the hillside under a tangle of vegetation that includes stinging nettle. (Beware, it is very painful! Use aloe or mugwort for relief.) Miners dug a pond on the hillside here, and it is jammed with cattails.

From the end of the road you must backtrack to Chorro Grande Trail to get back to the highway. (The trail seen heading almost straight up the south side of Reyes Peak here is old, heavily eroded and not used anymore.)

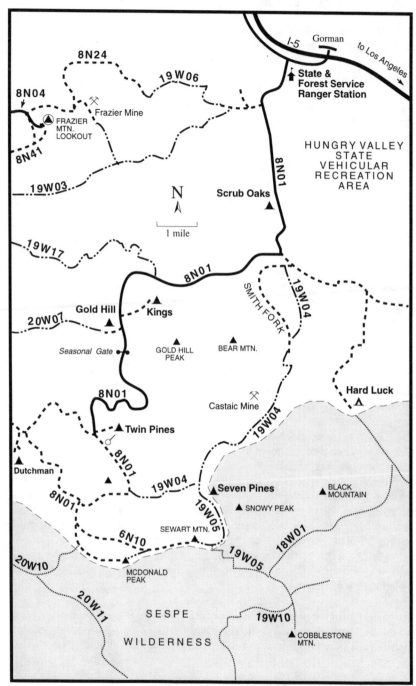

to Los Angeles

Gorman

I-5

8N24

19W06

8N04

Frazier Mine

FRAZIER
MTN.
LOOKOUT

8N41

State &
Forest Service
Ranger Station

HUNGRY VALLEY
STATE
VEHICULAR
RECREATION
AREA

19W03

N

1 mile

Scrub Oaks

8N01

19W17

8N01

SMITH FORK

19W04

Gold Hill

Kings

20W07

GOLD HILL
PEAK

BEAR MTN.

Seasonal Gate

Hard Luck

8N01

Castaic Mine

19W04

Twin Pines

8N01

Dutchman

19W04

Seven Pines

BLACK
MOUNTAIN

8N01

19W05

SNOWY PEAK

6N10

SEWART MTN.

18W01

20W10

MCDONALD
PEAK

19W05

19W10

20W11

SESPE

WILDERNESS

COBBLESTONE
MTN.

© F.E.P. 1993

CHAPTER 7   HUNGRY VALLEY / ALAMO MOUNTAIN
Hungry Valley, Alamo Mountain Road, Alamo Mountain Loop
Road, Sewart Mountain Road, Miller Jeep Road

Alamo Mountain is a massive peak with a somewhat rounded top. Its highest point is 7450 feet, but the road never gets higher than 7000 feet'. At this elevation snows occurs every year and sometimes remains for a long time. The best riding is in summer and fall. If you plan to camp during these warmer months, you still need to be prepared for cold nights on the mountain. Except for the noise and speed of motorcycles, this area has great riding. You get spectacular views of seldom-seen canyons from the higher elevations. Alamo Mountain is covered with huge trees, while Hungry Valley to the northeast is dry and desert-like.

There is much evidence of gold mining in some areas of the region. Located on the north slope of the mountain above Piru Creek, the Castaic Mine was the most extensive and successful one, with two tunnels totaling over 2200 feet in length. Mining continued here into the 1930s. Originally powered by a water wheel, the 5-stamp mill from this mine can now be seen in a historical museum in Santa Barbara. Gold panning is still a popular pastime along nearby streams.

Alamo Mountain is accessible by motor vehicle from Interstate 5 through the Hungry Valley State Vehicular Recreational Area (motorcycle & 4WD) on a generally paved road as far as the Gold Hill-Piru Creek crossing. Take Interstate 5 to Gorman (60 miles from Los Angeles, 40 miles from Bakersfield, and 70 miles from Ventura). Cross to the west side of I-5 opposite Gorman and go north on Peace Valley Road 1 mile. Turn left (west) at the SVRA Hungry Valley sign onto paved Gold Hill Road #8N01. A checkpoint kiosk just ahead is run by the state to collect fees for SVRA use. No fee is required to pass through to the National Forest beyond. Maps and current information are available from the State Ranger, and information is posted on large bulletin boards. Call ahead to check weather, closures, and special events scheduled here and in the National Forest: (805) 248-6447, P.O. Box 1360, Lebec, CA 93243-1360.

On Gold Hill Road at mile 5 there is an abrupt right turn. A dirt fork to the left is Hungry Valley Road, which leads to Snowy Creek Trail and farther on to Hard Luck Road. Go right and continue west on paved Gold Hill Road to the 10-mile mark at Piru Creek. A gate near the creek crossing is locked during stormy winter weather and when ice and snow are hazardous at higher elevations. From the base of Alamo Mountain, Road #8N01 twists and turns up the mountain's north side. Above Piru Creek, Gold Hill Road (formerly graded dirt) was paved in the fall of 1992.

Services and supplies are available only in Gorman on I-5. Most of the roads and trails in this area are open to motorcycles and all-terrain vehicles. Car camping with limited facilities is available at Kings Camp, Gold Hill Camp, Twin Pines and Dutchman camps on Alamo Mountain, and most sheltered spots in Hungry Valley (check with State Rangers).

Gold Hill Camp is located on a bluff above Piru Creek. The creek usually runs all year, although it's never very deep except during floods. Snow can occur here, but a lot of rain or snow is uncommon. Placer gold, washed downstream, is found along Piru Creek and in the bank under the bluff next to the camp. Panning and dredging along here is quite popular.

Kings Camp, at the end of Road #8N01A, offers tables and fire pits in a grove of trees. To reach the camp, turn east from Gold Hill Road at mile 10.25 on to paved Road #8N01A and continue 1/2 mile. Water is not available at this camp.

Hungry Valley

The 19,000-acre Hungry Valley State Vehicular Recreation Area (HV-SVRA) offers 2,000 acres of open riding area and over 80 miles of trails for all types of off-highway vehicles. This includes bicycles, and cyclists can find a wide variety of riding experiences here.

I am aware this land wasn't set aside for bicycling, but since bicycles have been declared vehicles for the purpose of keeping us out of wilderness areas, and since this is an off-highway vehicle area, why not take advantage of it? Sure, there are lots of motor vehicles zooming around, but the cyclist can still fit in. Ride during the week, in the early morning, or in winter when it's cold. At least here no one is liable to complain that you are going too fast or ruining the trails. You can't frighten the horses or hikers — I doubt you will ever see any.

For kamakazi descents, the motorcycle hill-climbing walls should be a thrill. (Trails signs rate the degree of difficulty.) Several trails continue into the Los Padres National Forest and provide longer, more remote rides, usually with more solitude than you get in the Recreation Area.

Hungry Valley has a desert-like appearance — dry with sparce vegetation. Summer days can be very hot. The 3500-foot elevation means many days of wind, and cold winter nights with occasional snow. I first became aware of the area through my interest in recreational gold prospecting. Gold is found on Frazier Mountain, along Piru Creek, and in the mountains on each side of Piru Creek near Gold Hill. Old mines and diggings — as well as current diggers — can be found throughout these parts. Much of my knowledge was passed on to me by James Young, who worked at the Castaic Mine during the Depression when he was in his early twenties. Mining, hunting, and ranching were the main activities then. Jim was a partner of Paul Meacham, and together they worked the mine. They went to town (Gorman) only one day a month for supplies.

Jim Young was always interested in the world around him, and 30 days at a time at the mine was too much isolation for him. So sometimes after work on Saturdays, he would walk to Gorman for a night out. When the town closed for the night, he would head back to the mine with a bottle of beer in his pocket, stories of world and local news in his head, and thoughts of renewed friendships to keep him company on the long, lonely hike. Arriving back at the mine by daybreak, he'd be thankful for Sunday off so he could sleep. Hiking to Gorman from the Castaic Mine is not an unpleasant walk, as I once found out when I was returning from a day's prospecting after a friend's car broke down not far from the mine. We walked out in the dark, and I thought about Jim Young's walks 50 years earlier. In the dark, the country probably looks much the same, but in daylight, I know for a fact there are some major changes — a paved road, power lines, and many, many motorcycle trails.

Alamo Mountain Road

Route/Trail: #8N01
Length: 7 miles one way
Level of Difficulty: Moderate; big climb at high elevation
Elevation: 4000' - 6500', 2500' diff.
Water: Piru Creek — doubtful quality; Twin Pines Camp — pipe spring
Parking: On flats north of Piru Creek near Gold Hill crossing
Campgrounds: Gold Hill and Kings camps
Nearest Services: Gorman

This recently paved (August 1992) road up Alamo Mountain is rideable uphill but is a long 7-mile climb. The road is open to all motor vehicles and sometimes can be busy. Early morning is the best time to ride, particularly on weekdays.

Twisting and turning up the north side of the mountain, the grade doesn't vary much and is rideable the whole way if you have the stamina for it. You pass by chaparral and juniper most of the way up, and pine trees begin occurring and about half way up. These get more numerous until at the top you are in a thick forest of pine. There is no water available until just below the Loop Road at the top. A short road to the east (left) that leads to Twin Pines Camp passes a water trough with water piped in from a nearby spring. Another spring is beside the Loop Road to the west, part way to Dutchman Camp.

If big climbs are not your thing, drive up, park, and ride the loop road around Alamo Mountain (see next ride description).

Alamo Mountain Loop Road

Route/Trail: #8N01
Length: 8 miles
Level of Difficulty: Easy, but remember at 6500' you won't have much air to breathe
Elevation: 6500' -7000'; 500' diff.
Water: Piped spring near Twin Pines Camp; spring beside the loop road about 1/2 mile west of Twin Pines Camp
Parking: Turnout near Twin Pines Camp
Campgrounds: Twin Pines and Dutchman drive-in camps
Nearest Services: Gorman

This road circles Alamo Mountain between 6500 feet and 7000 feet for 8 miles of easy riding in mature pine forest. The views from all sides of Alamo Mountain are splendid. Although you may drive a vehicle around the mountain on this road, riding a bicycle puts you more in touch with the surroundings.

As you are coming up the mountain, a short spur road to the east leads steeply down to Twin Pines Camp, just a little before the Loop Road begins. Dutchman Camp, 2.5 miles west on the loop road, is spread over a larger area with more level ground. No water is available near Dutchman Camp, though.

The easiest way to do this loop is to ride counter-clockwise, starting toward the west. The 2.5-mile ride out to Dutchman Camp meanders along the slopes, passing through groves of pines. The 200-foot elevation gain isn't difficult,

since it's done a little at a time. Where the road turns south, another lesser road heads farther east. This is the Miller Jeep Road #8N12 and it connects with the many double tracks to the campsites next to the loop. The sites are spread out in this open place among a few scattered pines of good size.

On the 3-mile stretch from the camp out to the south point of the loop road, you travel fairly level the first mile. The next 2 miles climb 250 feet, descend into a small canyon, climb again, and end at the same elevation as the camp. Rocks fall onto the road from the steeper slopes around the small canyon.

At the south point, Road #6N10 to McDonald Peak and Sewart Mountain descends steeply south. It's worthwhile to make the half-mile trip out to the ridge for the views down Alder Creek and out to the Sespe Narrows. Keep going south on the Loop Road without turning to the east or west. By going out this half mile you get most of the view afforded by doing the entire 6-mile round trip to Sewart Mountain (see next ride description). I highly recommend it if you have time while doing the loop.

The Loop Road is cut through the ridge here and turns sharply to the northeast. The view is into the upper parts of Snowy Creek Canyon, which starts from the south ridge of Alamo Mountain and curves around to the northeast. After riding northeast 0.7 mile from the south point on the Loop Road, you pass Snowy Creek Trail on the right. (Snowy Creek Trail is not recommended.) Continue on 1.8 miles, descending 300 feet, to complete your turn around the mountain and return to the starting point. The trees along this last section are a mixed forest of maples, oaks, and pines.

Sewart Mountain Road
Route/Trail: #6N10
Length: 3 miles
Water: None
Level of Difficulty: Moderate; steeper hills out near Sewart Mountain
Elevation: 6850' - 6400'; several times up and down on a ridge
Parking: Near Twin Pines Camp or along the Alamo Mountain Loop Road
Campgrounds: Twin Pines or Dutchman camps
Nearest Services: Gorman

Everyone who gets as far as the south point of Alamo Mountain Loop Road should consider at least taking the half-mile trip out to the ridge that connects McDonald Peak and Sewart Mountain. So many canyons, ridges, sandstone reefs, and peaks are visible from the ridge that I never have enough time to take it all in. The views are unique, especially south into the Sespe Narrows and to the Topa Topa wall, west of the narrows. Most of the land you see is in the Sespe Wilderness. The boundary runs along the south side of the ridge from east of McDonald Peak to Big Cedar Creek, then down that and Snowy Creek to Piru Creek.

Heading south off the Loop Road, be sure to keep control of your speed since the terrain below the road is steep and rocky. At the bottom of this descent, you pass a short spur road heading down toward the former Alamo Camp, west of this saddle. Beyond this spur the signed Sewart Mountain Road #6N10 crosses over into Snowy Canyon. It passes by McDonald Peak on the north and comes out of the canyon and onto the ridge east of the peak, avoiding climbs on the peak itself. This is a good way to return to the Loop Road. Keep right at the Sewart Road sign and climb steeply to the ridge here, rather rounded on top with rolling terrain. Take your time, since this is one of the most scenic places in the forest and an excellent rest and lunch stop. Riding east, you drop and climb over many peaks on the ridge, part of the way on a trail, before joining the road, which climbs back to the ridge east of McDonald Peak. There is a particularly steep place just before Sewart Mountain.

On the east side of Sewart Mountain, Big Cedar Creek Trail goes down into Snowy Creek Canyon. It is very steep and rough, and I don't recommend it. Return to Alamo Mountain Loop Road from Sewart Mountain by taking the road where it passes north of McDonald Peak and avoid the climbs on the ridge.

Miller Jeep Road

Route/Trail: # 8N12
Length: 3 miles
Level of Difficulty: Very difficult; steep, rutted rough road
Elevation: 6700' - 4300'; 2400' diff.
Water: None
Parking: Gold Hill Camp; Dutchman Camp on Alamo Mountain
Campgrounds: Dutchman Camp (upper roadhead); Sunset Camp at the bottom
Nearest Services: Gorman

This steep rocky road climbs a ridge from Lockwood Flat at Piru Creek to the Alamo Loop Road #8N01 on the west side of the mountain. But it is best traveled downhill, and you can do this as part of a loop trip or using a car shuttle. If you use only one vehicle, park at Gold Hill Camp and ride up Alamo Mountain Road and do this as a very strenuous loop. For a shuttle, your other vehicle can be parked at Dutchman Camp.

From Gold Hill Camp, ride or drive up Alamo Mountain on Road #8N01 and take the right (west) fork around the mountain 2.5 miles to Dutchman Camp. There the Miller Jeep Road leaves the Loop Road and passes just north of the camp. Follow it west and up a hill northwest of camp, where it will turn and steeply descend the north side of the mountain to Piru Creek. There you take Piru Creek Trail east, passing Lockwood Creek Road and Sunset Camp on the way to Gold Hill Camp.

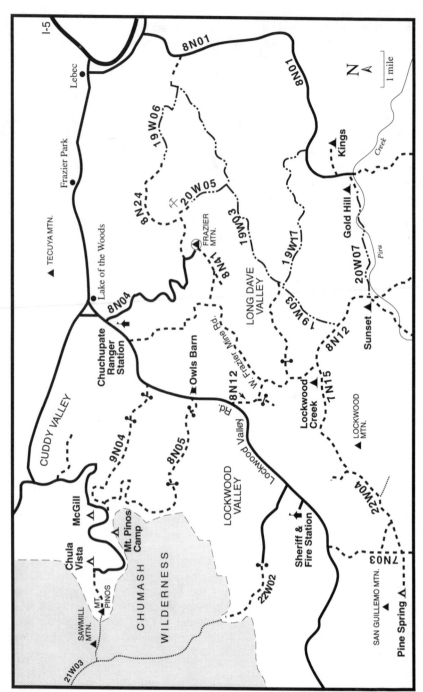

© F.E.P. 1993

CHAPTER 8   LOCKWOOD VALLEY
North Fork Lockwood Creek, Lockwood Creek Road, West Frazier Mine Road, Long Dave Valley Road, Long Dave Valley Trail, Piru Creek Trail

This wide valley with massive mountains rising over 8000 feet in the north and east is very different from the forest to the south. The valley floor at 5000 feet can be very cold in winter and usually has some snowfall but it doesn't last long. The nearby peaks can have snow patches lasting into May. Valley summers are pleasant with moderate temperatures. The vegetation consists of meadow grassland and sage with scattered clumps of pines.

Lockwood Valley Road is a paved road from Highway 33 to Interstate 5 through Lockwood Valley and the communities of Lake of the Woods and Frazier Park. Supplies are available there and at Lebec and Gorman on I-5. At the southwest end of the valley there is a Ventura County Sheriff's Substation and Fire Station (end of Chico Larson Way at mile 17.9 on Lockwood Valley Road). Kern County sheriff and fire stations are located in Frazier Park. Mt. Pinos Ranger District Headquarters is located a mile southwest of Lake of the Woods at the junction of Lockwood Valley Road and Frazier Mountain Road. Campfire permits, forest maps, books and pamphlets, road/trail conditions and closures, and other information is available here.

Wilderness legislation creating the Chumash Wilderness Area — encompassing land on Mt. Pinos and south and west of Mt. Abel — has closed some trails to bicycles. Also, owners and residents of private land in Seymour and Mill canyons no longer allow through traffic across their lands. You can ride down both of these canyon roads from the upper end near McGill Camp on Mt. Pinos, but you must turn back once you reach the private property.

North Fork Lockwood Creek
Route/Trail: #22W02
Length: 2.5 miles one way
Level of Difficulty: Easy
Elevation: 5450' - 6000'; 550' diff.
Water: Seasonal at the falls; road end
Parking: Along the paved Boy Scout Road, off pavement, near Plush Ranch and the gate, 3 miles from Lockwood Valley Road
Campgrounds: Nearest is Pine Spring off Mutau Road #7N03
Nearest Services: Lake of the Woods

From Lockwood Valley Road, mile 18.6, head northwest on Boy Scout Road, 3 miles to the gate. A sign at the gate gives directions. Ride through the Boy Scout Camp parking area, and continue straight ahead on the road at the far right side. Several stream crossings in the canyon are usually dry but they do wash out sometimes and flash floods occur during heavy thunderstorms. This road ends just below a large waterfall. You will have to walk upstream a short distance to look around a turn of the canyon to see the falls. The trail past enters the Chumash Wilderness there, and no bikes are allowed beyond that point.

Lockwood Creek Road
Route/Trail: #8N12
Length: 4 miles one way
Level of Difficulty: Moderate, with many difficult stream crossings
Elevation: 4800' - 4300', 500' diff.
Water: In creek, but of doubtful quality, so carry your own supplies
Parking: Large parking area next to the Road #8N12, 1.6 miles from Lockwood Valley Road
Campgrounds: Lockwood and Sunset trail camps along the creek
Nearest Services: Lake of the Woods

Go 5.5 miles southwest of Lake of the Woods on Lockwood Valley Road to mile 20.3 and take signed dirt road #8N12 to the south. At 0.8 mile, take the left fork and cross an often-dry creek. Head up a steep hill and pass the Forest Service gate. Going downhill again you pass, at 1.4 miles, West Frazier Mine Road on the left. Next you will come to a large parking area. At the parking area's lower side, the Lockwood Creek Road drops down into the stream and enters the narrow Lockwood Canyon headed south. (At the upper east end of the parking area is a Long Dave Valley Road; see ride description below.)

From here on, Road #8N12 is used mostly by 4WDs and motorcycles. It's rough and rocky in many places with a few short, steep hills. It keeps to the canyon bottom, and in some sections to the creek bed itself — as much in as out for the first mile. Expect to get your pedals wet. During storms and high runoff, it can be dangerous, so be prepared to turn back if necessary.

Lockwood Creek Trail Camp is 0.7 mile from the parking area and has four sites with tables and fireplaces among shade trees on the west side of the creek. Next you pass Yellowjacket Road #7N15, which enters the first canyon on the right (west) at 1.3 miles. Beyond here, Lockwood Canyon opens a little and travel is easier up out of the creek. Near the 2.5-mile point you pass Trail #19W03 into Long Dave Canyon on the left (east).

Below this junction Lockwood Creek Road stays to the east of the creek and is good for 0.8 mile. The creek makes a big loop around a ridge coming into the canyon from the west while the road cuts across and then drops steeply back down and crosses the creek again. Cottonwood trees grow along the creek above the loop, which is the abandoned site of Cottonwood Trail Camp. It was a good location when travel here was by foot or horseback, but off-highway vehicle travelers don't stop at this camp and it is seldom used now. The last part of the road to Sunset Trail Camp at Lockwood Flat near Piru Creek is much rougher, having been washed out in a flood that left long stretches of dry, rocky creek bed for a road. At Sunset Camp you can return back up Lockwood Canyon or continue on to Gold Hill Road by Piru Creek Trail #20W07.

West Frazier Mine Road

Route/Trail: Off-highway route #118
Length: 5 miles one way or part of a 11.4-mile loop
Level of Difficulty: Very difficult; rough, rocky road with very steep sections
Elevation: 5400' at Lockwood Valley Road; 6600' at high point; 5000' at Lockwood Creek Road #8N12
Water: None
Parking: Along Lockwood Valley Road 1/3 mile west of Chuchupate Ranger Station
Campgrounds: None
Nearest Services: Lake of the Woods

Experienced riders can test their skill and stamina on this road through rugged terrain. It's best to start from the eastern end near the ranger station and ride to Lockwood Creek Road #8N12. You can then return by the paved highway back to your start for a total loop of 11.4 miles.

This road is unmarked at its beginning 1/3 mile west of the Chuchupate Ranger Station, where you head south from the paved road. You cross the eastern side of a field and then turn west, with some rough traveling to rejoin the old route that used to cross the field directly through private property. Keep west and avoid some confusing side routes on the way to the old road there. Next you turn south and climb steeply past a seasonal closure gate. The first 1.5 miles is a steep ascent to where West Frazier Tie Road joins in from above, and there is another seasonal gate there. The rest of this road is mostly downhill, with many very steep sections. The vegetation consists of mixed chaparral and pines. From the Tie Road on, you will be traveling west along the north side of Frazier Mountain toward Lockwood Creek. The road runs out onto a ridge and then turns back to the southeast to descend into and cross two small canyons. In the first one, right at the switchback by the wash, is an old mine tunnel. It is partially caved in at the entrance, blocking the water that drains out and flooding the floor. Mines are dangerous; old mines are deadly. Look, but keep out!

This road alternates between awful and pretty good with the last 1.5 miles pretty decent. The last half mile is down in a canyon bottom and fairly flat. Several unimproved campsites here are used often by 4WD enthusiasts. When you get to the end of the Mine Road you will be at Lockwood Creek Road #8N12. The paved Lockwood Valley Road can be reached by turning right and riding north 1.4 miles. At the highway, turn right again and 5 miles east is your starting point.

Long Dave Valley Road

Route/Trail: Off-highway Road #123
Length: 4 miles one way
Level of Difficulty: Moderate
Elevation: 4800' - 5900'; 1100' diff.
Water: None
Parking: Lockwood Creek Road #8N12 parking area, 1.6 miles from Lockwood Valley Road
Campgrounds: None
Nearest Services: Lake of the Woods

This is a nice way to explore Long Dave Valley, situated on the southwest side of Frazier Mountain. The grade up is even, and although somewhat steep, it is rideable by strong riders with low gears. It's 2.5 miles uphill to the ridge, and the last mile is less steep. Remember that this road is access to private land in Long Dave Valley and is frequently used by motor vehicles.

Start from the parking area 1.6 miles down Lockwood Creek Road #8N12 from Lockwood Valley Road. Head northeast uphill away from Lockwood Creek. At the upper end of the parking area, keep to the right and follow the road that heads into a canyon towards the east. At about 0.7 mile is a large gate with a sign prohibiting 4WD vehicles past that point. From the high point on the ridge, there isn't much view into the valley, but by continuing on another 1/2 mile down an easy descent, a viewpoint is reached where the valley and road into it can be plainly seen. To the southwest through Long Dave Canyon is a view out across Piru Creek, Mutau Flat, and clear to the Topa Topa Mountains. At the road end is a wooden gate to private land. The Tejon Trail starts up steeply on the left (northeast), Gold Hill Trail goes up to a ridge on the southeast, and Long Dave Canyon Trail heads to the right (southwest) down through pine trees.

You can return to Lockwood Creek parking area by Long Dave Valley Road. Or for a much tougher ride, take the tough and narrow Long Dave Canyon Trail, which connects to Lockwood Creek Road and provides a 9.2-mile loop trip for experienced riders expecting a challenge (see next ride description).

Long Dave Valley Trail

Route/Trail: #19W03
Length: 2.7 miles one way; usually done as part of a 9.2-mile loop
Level of Difficulty: Very difficult, rough trail
Elevation: 5500' - 4500'; 1000' diff.
Water: None
Parking: Lockwood Creek Road #8N12 parking area, 1.6 miles from Lockwood Valley Road
Campgrounds: Lockwood Creek Trail Camp
Nearest Services: Lake of the Woods

Special Caution: This is a designated motorcycle route; look for safe passing places

Start by taking Long Dave Valley Road to Long Dave Valley Trail. Then for this 9.2-mile loop, travel down the canyon and return back to the Lockwood Creek parking area. Some parts of the trail are nice; there are even interesting things to see — like old car parts and mining equipment at 0.6 mile where the Gold Hill Trail #19W17 comes in. Repeatedly crossing the creek and clambering over rocky drop-offs in the middle section is tiring. It's soon past, though, and the lower canyon opens up a little with the trail leveling out for much better riding. Right at the end you come out of the canyon on a short road that connects with Lockwood Creek Road #8N12. Turn right (north) to return to the parking area.

Piru Creek Trail
Route/Trail: #20W07
Length: 4 miles one way (the section from Gold Hill Road to Lockwood Flat)
Level of Difficulty: Experienced trail riders only (steep drop-off beside trail)
Elevation: 4000' - 4300'; 300' diff.
Water: Piru Creek, but the quality is questionable
Parking: Gold Hill Camp above Piru Creek Bluff. Take a dirt road to the right of a large, metal information sign about 10.5 miles along Gold Hill Road #8N01. Keep to the right and beware of loose soil on lesser traveled paths.
Campgrounds: Gold Hill Camp
Nearest Services: Gorman

Special Caution: This is a designated motorcycle route; look for safe passing places

Piru Creek Trail #20W07 leaves Gold Hill Camp headed uphill to the west and can be seen crossing steep slopes northwest of camp. This first climb gets you above cliffs upstream from the camp where Piru Creek flows through a short gorge. Here the trail is narrow with extreme drop-offs toward the creek. If in doubt of your ability on this section, walk or go back. After passing this tough mile, the trail drops down to the creek and is much easier, except for loose sand. Sunset Trail Camp is at Lockwood Flat at the end of this 4-mile section of trail where you connect to Lockwood Creek Road.

Piru Creek Trail continues past this junction to connect with the Miller Jeep Road to Alamo Mountain. The only way to travel farther west is in the creek bed during periods of low water. West of the jeep road the Piru Creek Trail has been completely washed out by the river.

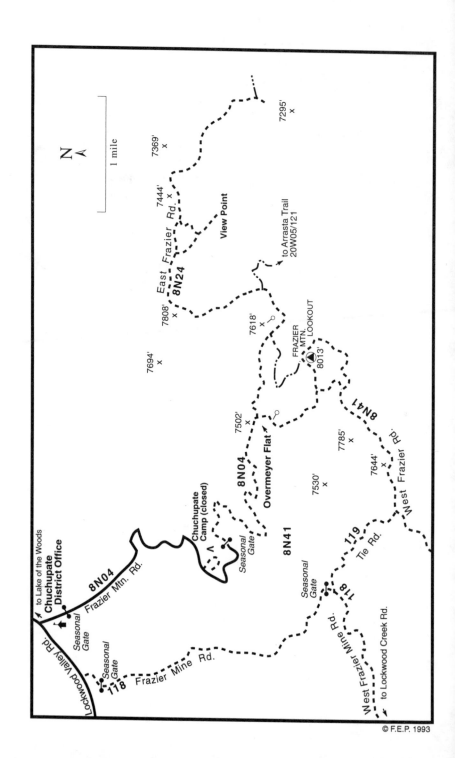

© F.E.P. 1993

CHAPTER 9   FRAZIER MOUNTAIN
Frazier Mountain Road, West Frazier Road, East Frazier Road

Good dirt roads and thick pine forests create a tranquil, relaxed mood while riding on the wide ridges of this high mountain. The trees muffle and block sound, so talking with hushed voices seems right here, like in a church or library. Broken tops on the largest trees attest to the power of wind, lightning, and heavy snow, but on a bright summer day when the heat is tempered by the 7500-foot elevation, this is a gentle wilderness. Most of the views through the trees are spectacular. The best view, of course, is at the fire lookout on the very top of the mountain at 8013 feet — one of the few manned lookouts left in the southern forest. Visitors are welcome, but remember every day is a working day. Keep visits and distractions short.

The main access road up the mountain is paved for 3 miles to over 7000 feet. A good graded dirt road continues on to the fork at Overmeyer Flat, a good parking place. East Frazier Road to the left is 5.2 miles long. On the right, it's 1.6 miles to the lookout on the mountain top and 2 miles back by a loop road south of the lookout. West Frazier Road #8N41, also to the right, is 3.5 miles long and connects with the very steep and rough West Frazier Tie Road down the north side of the mountain.

Special Hazards: Spring and summer thunderstorms are common with possible heavy rain and the danger of lightning on high places. In storms, keep away from tall trees and metal structures like the lookout and nearby radio towers. Heavy winter snow occurs, and strong winds cause whiteouts and severe wind chill. In the shade at this high elevation, snow and ice can last a long time. Check conditions at the ranger station on the way up or call ahead.

Frazier Mountain Road
Route/Trail: #8N04
Length: 7.4 miles one way
Level of Difficulty: Moderate
Elevation: 5200' - 8013', 2913' diff.
Water: None; signs posted at the springs indicate hazardous water quality
Parking: Parking area at Chuchupate Ranger Station (check at the desk)
Campgrounds: None
Nearest Services: Lake of the Woods

Go west 0.9 mile from Lake of the Woods on Lockwood Valley Road. Signs here direct you south to Frazier Mountain Road and Chuchupate Ranger Station. The station is near the highway and the best source of current information. If you park at the station and bicycle up the mountain, be sure to check at the desk for all day or long term parking. The parking in front of the office is for office visits only.

As you do this ride up the mountain, be sure to stop and survey the distant terrain. Use a map and compass to become familiar with the features of the area and it will help you find your way.

For the first mile you climb steadily south on the road past chaparral and scattered pines. The road turns to the left a little and gets less steep at two houses — one stone, the other of logs. At 1.5 miles, the first switchback turns to the right and cuts along the mountainside, which becomes much steeper. Camp buildings at 2.0 miles are on the left beyond a meadow full of grasses and wildflowers with water flowing out and across the road. Chuchupate Camp is at 2.5 miles, closed due to ground squirrels infested with fleas carrying bubonic plague.

Switchback again and turn left to double back above the camp, and at 3.0 miles the pavement ends at a seasonal closure gate. The dirt road past here is rocky but good. You keep heading southeast, and at 4.3 miles the road improves. Nearing the top, the trees are bigger and shade the road. At Overmeyer Flat, 5.8 miles, the road forks with East Frazier Road #8N24 branching left.

Keep to the right fork on Frazier Mountain Road for a nice half-mile ride to the lookout, which loops back to Overmeyer Flat with many scenic surprises. From Overmeyer Flat, it's 1.1 miles to the lookout junction. The left fork leads up 1/2 mile to the lookout, which is situated amid an amazing array of antennas on the mountain top. You may return to Overmeyer Flat by continuing past the lookout, heading south on a road that behaves itself, and traveling in a half circle to the west for 0.6 mile to West Frazier Road #8N41. Turn right, travel 0.3 mile and you will be back at the fork where you turned up to the lookout. Keep straight ahead, and 1.1 miles of riding will put you back at Overmeyer Flat.

West Frazier Road
Route/Trail: #8N41
Length: 2.4 miles one way
Level of Difficulty: Moderate; steep, rough road last half mile
Elevation: 7900' - 7000'; 900' diff.
Water: None
Parking: Overmeyer Flat (add 1.1 miles); Frazier Mountain Lookout (add 0.5 mile)
Campgrounds: None
Nearest Services: Lake of the Woods

Include the loop around the lookout when you ride out along the West Frazier Road. The view there is so spectacular, whereas the thick forest blocks almost all the views on the West Ridge Road. If you start from Overmeyer Flat, go past the roads to the lookout by keeping to the right. Then on the way back, go up to the lookout on the road from the south circling counter-clockwise. Ride the same counter-clockwise direction when parking near the lookout. The approach to the mountain top is easier from the south.

Starting from Overmeyer Flat, ride up the right fork at the nearby sign. The road turns southwest as it climbs along the slopes through pine forest. A spring at a stone water catchment is labeled as bad water. Here it's a good graded road, and at 1.1 miles you will pass the main access road to the lookout. Signs at this left turn point the way, 1/2 mile up to the east. Keep riding straight ahead, and 0.3 mile farther another lesser traveled road also heads east to the lookout. Take this one when you return. It climbs in a 0.6-mile half circle up to the lookout.

You will be descending toward the west along the ridge. Keep in mind that you have to come back up the same way and it will take longer. The ride is through thick forest with some small open areas. At 2.9 miles from Overmeyer Flat, or 2.3 miles from the lookout, West Frazier Tie Road branches off to the north. It's nearly level on the part you see, but it soon plunges down the mountain. Riding out on that level part is easier, however, than continuing west on West Frazier Road, which drops steeply and is rough the last 0.6 mile. No matter which way you go, you need to backtrack to return to the lookout.

East Frazier Road
Route/Trail: #8N24
Length: 5.2 miles one way
Level of Difficulty: Moderate
Elevation: 7500' start; 7800' high point; 7350 end; 450' diff.
Water: None; hazardous water signs posted at the springs
Parking: Overmeyer Flat on Road #8N04
Campgrounds: None
Nearest Services: Lake of the Woods

This is a good ride for a hot summer day. It is usually cooler at this altitude and there is plenty of shade on the road, which travels along a broad ridge covered with pine forest. There are some less-traveled side roads and many clearings where you can get off the main road and enjoy the solitude. Bring a lunch, your camera, binoculars, a book, harmonica, or even a hammock. This is such a peaceful place that you should plan time for quiet, relaxing activities to experience the mood of the mountain. Most of the ride is easy, but there are a few short steep hills where you can expend some energy.

Park along Frazier Mountain Road at Overmeyer Flat, ride up to the signed road fork and go left on East Frazier Road #8N24. You will continue to climb moderately for a half mile around the north side of the mountain. The upper end of a canyon is below to the east, and the road descends slightly toward the ridge at the head of this canyon. A water trough with water piped to it from a spring can be seen in the canyon below (water quality unknown). Near the bottom of this hill, at 0.9 mile, a rough, steep road heads up the northeast side of the mountain to the lookout. You descend to about 1.1 miles and then climb until you reach the Arrasta Trail #20W05/OHV #121 on the right (mile 1.5).

The road continues east on the ridge, dropping and climbing through thick forest. At 3.2 miles, a double track to the right crosses the ridge for 0.45 mile to dead end at an overlook viewpoint. From this promontory you can look west and see the microwave towers near the lookout. (On the way back, at 0.2 mile from the main road, another double track heads east; at 3.5 miles a double track on the right seems to head back up toward the road to the viewpoint. These two may connect, but I haven't tried it.) The main road crosses to the north side of the ridge so you can see out toward Bakersfield and down to Frazier Park. Just past that at 3.6 miles the road becomes divided while climbing a short hill.

Turning southeast and keeping on the ridge top, you pass the East Frazier Trail #19W06/OHV #120 at 5.1 miles. In this area there are many viewing places between the trees where you can see out across the Antelope Valley to Lancaster. The road descends more to the south and ends at a turn-around circle, 5.2 miles from Overmeyer Flat. For an easier trip, skip the last steep rocky descents and turn around at 5.0 miles.

If you want a more strenuous ride, go up to the lookout first on Road #8N04 rather than turning onto East Frazier Road. From the lookout, take the trail to the northwest, which heads down the mountain to the north, turns east, and then joins East Frazier Road 0.9 mile from its start at Frazier Mountain Road.

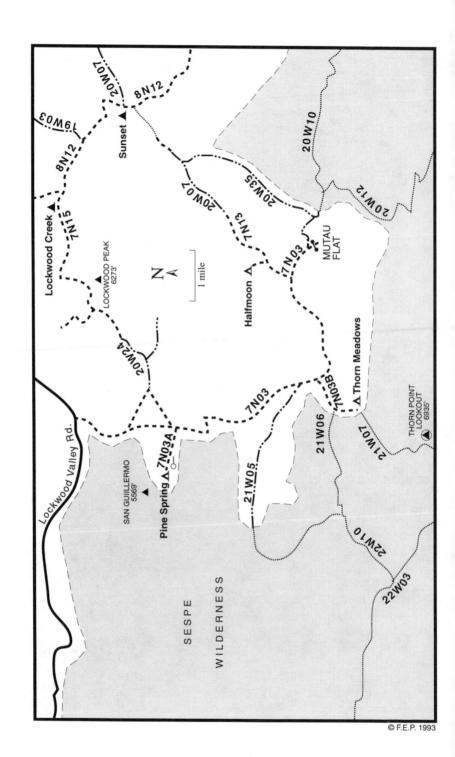

© F.E.P. 1993

CHAPTER 10   THORN MEADOWS
Mutau / Grade Valley Road, Piano Box Loop Road, Yellow Jacket Trail, Piru Creek Road, Mutau Flat Road, Mutau Creek Trail, Thorn Meadow Road

This area of excellent summer riding is the best place for beginners due to its many miles of easy-to-ride dirt roads. Thorn Meadows gets it name from the extensive wild roses growing here. At higher elevations, the many stands of large conifers, open meadow lands, and roads and trails with few steep climbs make this one of the best mountain bike areas around.

Drive-in campsites at Thorn Meadows, Pine Springs and Halfmoon camps are accessible by auto over graded dirt road #7N03 (Grade Valley Road) in summer and fall. During winter and spring the area is subject to snow and washouts. Due to the remoteness of this area, only vehicles in good working order with plenty of fuel, tools, and spare parts should come here; it's best to travel with two or more vehicles. The nearest supplies can be obtained at Lake of the Woods or Frazier Park east on Lockwood Valley Road towards Interstate 5.

In the Thorn Meadows area are the headwaters of Piru Creek — all streams here drain into Piru Creek, which flows east to Pyramid Lake near Interstate 5.

Emergency help: Ventura County Fire Department and Sheriff's Station (805-245-3829) in Lockwood Valley at end of Chico Larson Way (0.4 miles). Chico Larson Way is at mile 17.9 on Lockwood Valley Road, 1.5 miles east of Grade Valley Road.

The Los Padres National Forest, Mt. Pinos District Ranger Office is at Chuchupate Ranger Station on Frazier Mountain Road, 0.9 miles west of Lake of the Woods (at mile 26, Lockwood Valley Road). For 24-hour taped recreation information call (805) 245-3449.

Drive-in campsites:
Pine Springs — on a hillside among trees; has 8 sites, tables, fire pits, outhouse. A once developed spring in the creek bed is now in disrepair.
Thorn Meadows — 3 sites, tables, fire pits, outhouse. There may be water in the creek. Two campsites are located at a turnaround where lights at night will shine into your camp. It's not a very attractive place. The third site is west across a small stream and under a large spreading tree. It's the best camping at this location.
Halfmoon Camp — 10 sites, tables, fire pits, his & hers outhouses. No water. It is next to Piru Creek, normally a meager stream through sandy flats and not recommended for drinking without treatment by boiling or filtration. This camp is on a well-shaded flat above the creek in a grove of large pines.

Piano Box Loop Overflow Camp — undeveloped sites on the southeast part of loop; no water, no facilities. But it is an attractive area with some large trees and sites at flat places along the road.

Although enough rain and snow falls each year to allow large trees to grow and flourish here, there is very little surface runoff due to porous soils. So plan to bring your own supply of water to all of these camps. About 1 gallon per person per day is a safe estimate. Use more than one container in case of spills or leaks.

Mutau / Grade Valley Road

Route/Trail: #7N03 (graded auto road)
Length: 14 miles one way; you can bike back at any point
Level of Difficulty: Novice; just go easy on the long grade
Elevation: 5800' - 4700'; 1100' diff.
Water: None
Parking: Start at Lockwood Valley Road, mile 16.4
Campgrounds: Any of the areas listed in the opening remarks in this chapter
Nearest Services:
Lake of the Woods

Grade Valley Road #7N03 climbs 455 feet steeply in 1.6 miles from Lockwood Valley Road to reach terrain that is like a rolling plateau. At 2.3 and 2.8 miles, Piano Box Loop Road goes to the east, and at 2.9 miles Road #7N03A leads west to Pine Springs Camp, 1 mile uphill. Near 3.6 miles the descent to Grade Valley begins winding down the mountainside, and you have an extensive view of large meadows, forested hills, mountains, and canyons. If you are driving into this area, consider letting those passengers with bikes get out at this point and ride on from here. It's 1000 feet downhill to Piru Creek — just past the corral at the Fish Bowls trailhead, you cross Piru Creek at mile 7.0. Here the signed Thorn Meadow Road #7N03B is to the right. You cross Piru Creek again and travel beside it the next 5 miles. Piru Creek meanders along the wide canyon bottom with very little gradient. You ride on light sandy soil; it's easy and pleasant with an open landscape of scattered pines, brush and sandstone outcroppings. At the 12-mile point you cross Piru Creek again and it's 2 more miles up to the road end at Mutau Flat. Or take the left fork across the creek again on Piru Creek Road #7N13 and ride 1/2 mile to Halfmoon Camp.

Piano Box Loop
Route/Trail: Unnumbered
Length: 2.5 miles plus 0.5 miles on Grade Valley Road #7N03
Level of Difficulty: Easy; novice
Elevation: 5750' - 5550'; 200' diff.
Water: None
Parking: Along Grade Valley Road
Campgrounds: Pine Springs; Piano Box Loop (undeveloped sites)
Nearest Services: Lake of the Woods

This loop starts and ends on the east side of Grade Valley Road at mile 2.3 and 2.8 and joins Yellow Jacket Trail #7N15/#20W24 at its easternmost point. This very pleasant, short, easy road is good for beginners. If you're unsure about exploring it by bike, you can drive it by car; just don't drive down the Yellow Jacket Trail to the east — the trail isn't marked and it can be confusing. *Do not take any east forks,* just keep turning to the west and back towards Grade Valley Road.

Yellow Jacket Trail
Route/Trail: #20W24 / #7N15
Length: 7.5 miles one way
Level of Difficulty: Moderate; loose sandy spots, rough and rocky at trail ends
Elevation: 4650' - 550'; 900' diff.
Water: Springs at creek
Parking: Grade Valley Road #7N03; Piano Box Loop Road; Lockwood Creek Road #8N12
Campgrounds: Pine Springs Camp; Piano Box Loop (undeveloped sites)
Nearest Services: Lake of the Woods

Both ends of this combination road/trail are rough, but the middle 5 miles are wonderful. Unexpected meadows, some groves of large pines, and a good road are among the pleasant surprises there. Go in from Piano Box Loop and return, or ride on through to Lockwood Creek Road leaving a second vehicle at the far end of the ride (Lockwood Creek Road parking area, 1.3 miles from the lower end of Yellow Jacket Trail).

If you're up to it, ride this as part of a 16-mile loop. Park at Lockwood Valley Road and Grade Valley Road. Ride up Grade Valley Road, turn left onto Piano Box Loop, and continue on Yellow Jacket Trail to Lockwood Creek Road. Turn left there and head upstream to the highway and return to the starting point on the paved road. On this loop, you have 4.9 miles of paved road, 2.0 miles of single track, and 9.1 miles of dirt road.

At the easternmost turn of Piano Box Loop, Yellow Jacket Trail continues east as a road. It quickly deteriorates into a trail during a steep descent into Guillermo Creek. Just east of that creek bed, Sheep Creek Trail #20W18 branches off to the south and climbs over the ridge. At this junction, you continue east (left) and climb on a single track past some rough spots for another 1/4 mile. (Sheep Creek Trail used to connect to Piru Creek, but now it fades out well short of there.) At 2.0 miles you will be on a narrow dirt road headed east. After crossing a low saddle, the road begins its descent to the east. For the next few miles you will pass several big meadows. In the middle of this area, at 3.3 miles and among some of the largest pines, a spur road to the left through a grove of trees dead ends after 0.7 mile at a bluff overlooking Guillermo Creek and Lockwood Creek — an interesting and easy side trip out and back.

Water can often be seen at springs and in the creek at 3.9 miles. You cross a very large meadow on loose gravel and then travel along the meadow's east side to where you enter the narrow canyon section of this trail. Having traveled 5 miles over fairly level and good road/trail, this is a good place to turn back if you don't plan to continue through to Lockwood Creek.

From here you travel through pinyon pine forest mixed with chaparral, crossing the creek many times. Water flows in the creek from springs in the canyon at 5.75 miles. High water flows have left loose sand, gravel, and rocks in the road the last 2 miles to Lockwood Creek. The 1.3 miles to the parking area up Lockwood Creek Road are very rough, right in the stream, and high water can make travel here unsafe.

Piru Creek Road
Route/Trail: #7N13/#20W07
Length: 6 miles one way
Level of Difficulty: Moderate on the road; more difficult on the trail
Elevation: 4700' - 4400'; 300' diff.
Water: At Mutau Creek (none at Halfmoon)
Parking: Near Halfmoon Camp (do not block roads)
Campgrounds: Halfmoon Camp
Nearest Services: Lake of the Woods

The roads and trails here have deteriorated from erosion and lack of maintenance. From Halfmoon Camp to the Kinkaid Cabin site, where the road becomes a trail, the road crosses the creek many times, and for long stretches you travel in the shallow (or dry) stream. With almost no hills here, the only difficulty is loose sand, but much of the time there is a lot of it. Gold miners were active here in the 1930s, and even now part-time prospectors try their luck panning near Sheep Creek.

Travel is much harder past the road on the trail. The river banks are higher and steeper, and at each crossing you drop and climb the steep, rocky banks. There are many crossings. Finally you make the last crossing where Mutau Creek comes in, and where water is usually flowing. Just up from the creek is the junction with Mutau Creek Trail #20W35.

Travel farther east on the Piru Creek Trail just isn't practical because the trail is completely washed out. The only way to get through to Lockwood Creek Road is to keep in the stream bed about 2 of the next 3 miles.

Mutau Flat Road
Route/Trail: #7N03
Length: 2 miles
Level of Difficulty: Easy motor road for beginning riders
Elevation: 4700' - 4900'; 200' diff.
Water: None
Parking: Along Road #7N03, at turnout at the junction of #7N03 and #7N13, or at Halfmoon Camp
Campground: Halfmoon Camp
Nearest Services: Lake of the Woods

Mutau Road to the locked gate at Mutau Flats is an easy uphill ride with 200 feet of gain in about 2 miles — good road through pine forest. At the end of the road there is a fine view of Mutau Flats, an unusually level area of meadow (about 1 square mile) used for grazing cattle. The meadow is private property. At this point, you can also see past the flats to Sespe Canyon and Topa Topa Peak.

If you wish to go farther, take the motorcycle trail east from the parking area above the locked gate. This trail is fairly level for 3/4 mile and then it drops down to the banks of Mutau Creek. At 1.08 miles from the beginning of this trail is the junction with Mutau Creek Trail #20W35. The Sespe Wilderness boundary is on the south side of Mutau Creek. Bicycles are no longer allowed on Little Mutau Creek Trail #20W10 or Johnston Ridge Trail #20W12 to Sespe Hot Springs.

Mutau Creek Trail
Route/Trail: #20W35
Length: 4 miles one way; best as part of a 13.5-mile loop
Level of Difficulty: Downhill; moderate
Elevation: 4800' - 4400'; 400' diff.
Water: Carry adequate supplies. Treat all spring water.
Parking: Locked gate at end of Mutau Road #7N03. For a loop trip, park near Halfmoon Camp
Campgrounds: Halfmoon Camp
Nearest Services: Lake of the Woods

On the unmarked motorcycle trail from the parking area near Mutau Road locked gate at Mutau Flats, ride 1.08 miles to junction of Little Mutau Creek Trail #20W10 and Mutau Creek Trail #20W35. Take Mutau Creek Trail east (left) along Mutau Creek. This trail is used by motorcyclists and the dirt is very loose in some spots; however, the downhill isn't too difficult.

This is a pleasant canyon to explore; it comes out at Piru Creek Trail #20W07, which is more of a 4WD road than an actual trail. From the junction ride up (southwest) Piru Creek Trail #20W07 to Piru Creek Road #7N13 to Halfmoon Camp. This makes a good loop trip when you park or camp at Halfmoon Camp, reversing the Piru Creek Road ride described earlier in this chapter. (It's 2.5 miles from the camp up #7N13 and #7N03 to the Mutau Road locked gate.)

Thorn Meadow Road
Route/Trail: #7N03B
Length: 1.5 miles one way
Level of Difficulty: Easy; good graded road
Elevation: 4800' - 5000'; 200' diff.
Water: No reliable source
Parking: At turnouts on Grade Valley Road or Thorn Meadow Road
Campgrounds: Thorn Meadows
Nearest Services: Lake of the Woods

After descending through Grade Valley on Grade Valley Road, you come to Piru Creek and cross it at mile 7.0. There are two crossings close together, and between them signed Thorn Meadow Road #7N03B starts west. On #7N03B you soon cross the South Fork Piru Creek and have an easy 1.5-mile ride to Thorn Meadows, named after the thickets of wild rose bushes growing along the creek. (As you turn to the south you pass the Cedar Creek trailhead. This very popular trail is now closed to bicycles because it falls within the wilderness boundary, which is on the west side of the road.

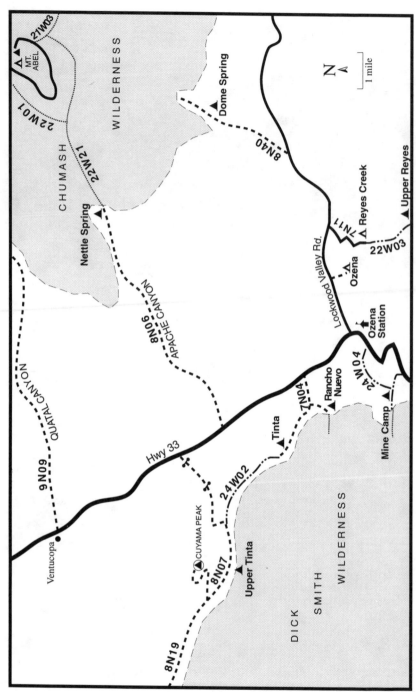

© F.E.P. 1993

CHAPTER 11   CUYAMA
East Dry Canyon Road, Tinta Canyon Road, Tinta Canyon Trail, Apache Canyon Road, Bear Canyon Trail

Looking down from Highway 33 at Pine Mountain Summit, the Cuyama River and the eroded hills below and to the east look like some kind of badlands, an impressive, desolate scene. The Cuyama River is usually a wide, flat, dry wash. The hills are sparsely covered, with light brown being the prominent color. The only really green areas are irrigated alfalfa fields near the river.

The best seasons to ride here are winter and early spring, when the higher elevations have snow and are cold. In summer, Cuyama is very hot and dry, and you must bring plenty of water. Also, be wary of driving your motor vehicle in soft sandy soils. There are drive-in camps at Ozena and Reyes Creek, as well as at Tinta Camp, Rancho Nuevo, Dome Springs in Dry Canyon and Nettle Springs in Apache Canyon (more rustic). Check local conditions at Ozena Forest Service Station on Highway 33 near Lockwood Valley Road.

East Dry Canyon Road
Route/Trail: #8N40
Length: 3 miles one way
Level of Difficulty: Easy
Elevation: 4000' - 4600'; 600' diff.
Water: None
Parking: Along Lockwood Valley Road at mile 6.4, or at Dome Springs Camp
Campgrounds: Dome Springs; Ozena; Reyes Creek
Nearest Services: Halfway Station Cafe; Ventucopa; New Cuyama

Ride up East Dry Canyon 3 miles to Dome Springs Camp on graded Road #8N40 and enjoy the much eroded landscape. Like many desert areas, Dry Canyon has some surprises — many trees and lots of plant life. Dome Springs Camp is located in a grove of pines, shaded and very nice; it's a drive-in camp with tables, fire pits and an outhouse. This is a good ride for beginners and those who are in no hurry and want to take it easy. East Dry Canyon rewards slow riders who have time to observe nature.

Tinta Canyon Road
Route/Trail: #7N04
Length: 3 miles one way
Level of Difficulty: Easy
Elevation: 3450' - 3600'; 150' diff.
Water: None
Parking: At the trailhead by the wilderness sign and map or the Halfway Station Cafe, 100 yards north on Highway 33
Campgrounds: Tinta; Rancho Nuevo
Nearest Services: Halfway Station Cafe; Ventucopa; New Cuyama

Most of this road is well graded and in fine shape. It's suitable for cars except that first you must cross the wide, flat Cuyama River. The water, when there is any, is usually shallow. The loose sand in the river bed here always makes me nervous about driving my car over it. And it's so far across that by the time I am halfway I am ready to promise never to try it again if I can only get out without getting stuck. Of course if you have 4WD you can go farther and get stuck in the very worst places. Nice thing about a bicycle is you can always pick it up and carry it.

This remote area doesn't usually get a lot of traffic, but because vehicles stir up clouds of dust, the best time to ride this road is during the week or when the way across the river is too rough for cars but okay for bicycles. Flash floods do occur here, and it's best to wait for the water to go down before crossing. If you are on the west side when a flood comes and have to get back, you can hike upstream on the west bank about 2 miles to the highway bridge.

One mile from the highway, a left off Road #7N04 heads south into Rancho Nuevo Canyon. It's 1/2 mile to the camp at the end of the road. Straight ahead on Road #7N04 it's two miles to Tinta Camp, also at the end of the road. It's not a very good camp, since the turnaround is right at the campsites and the designated motorcycle trail, Tinta Canyon Trail #24W02, is situated between them.

Tinta Canyon Trail
Route/Trail: #24W02/#8N07
Length: 7 miles one way
Level of Difficulty: Moderate to hard
Elevation: 3600' - 4800';1200' diff.
Water: From stream in canyon
Parking: Tinta Camp; Tinta roadhead (mile 50 on Highway 33)
Campgrounds: Tinta Camp; Upper Tinta Trail Camp
Nearest Services: Halfway Station Cafe; Ventucopa; New Cuyama
Special Caution: This is a designated motorcycle route, so look for safe passing places

Although it has lots of easy grade, recent washouts and brush growth have made this trail much more difficult than it used to be. Right out of Tinta Camp the trail stays close to the stream for 1/2 mile, then switchbacks up the north side of the canyon to get above a narrow, steep gorge. The switchback section is short (0.2 mile) and not very steep, but the next part is steep until at 1.0 mile you level out on the rim of the gorge. At 1.5 miles the gorge is behind you and you descend to the canyon bottom.

From here on the trail climbs gradually near the stream and is easier except where side gulches have cut through the trail. You have to climb in and out of these carrying your bicycle. The stream has a fair amount of water, and the trail crosses it several times. Brush is a problem near the stream. One last steep hill (it's short) and you are at the upper end of the 3.8-mile single track trail, where it joins a road that comes up Brubaker Canyon. This Road #8N07 is blocked at a locked gate near the Brubaker Ranch below. It climbs up over a saddle into Tinta Canyon, meets the trail, and continues up Tinta Canyon as a poor double track road — but a great trail. It has a slight grade that is easy to ride, and the brush is back far enough to not be a bother.

At 5.6 miles Upper Tinta Trail Camp — with one table and two stoves — is set among oak trees on a rise just left of the road. Near there are several creek crossings and some of them have water much of the time. The last 1/2 mile is rougher due to rocks left in the road by flood waters. A gate at 7.0 miles marks the end of Road #8N07. The Cuyama Peak Lookout service road passes here from West Dry Canyon.

The road up to the lookout is graded often and is in very good shape. It also climbs 1075 feet in 1.5 miles — very steep. If you have the time and energy, the view is worth the effort (this is one of the few old lookouts left standing). Unless you are prepared for a long loop, ride back the way you came in.

Strong riders may be interested in the loop option. From the end of Road #8N07 (at the turnoff to the lookout), continue west on West Dry Canyon Road #8N19 down to Santa Barbara Canyon and then take Road #9N11 north to Highway 33. These down-canyon roads are excellent riding. The return on Highway 33 is mostly level with a few rolling hills. Small stores, bars, and gas stations can be found near Ventucopa along the highway. Total distance for the loop is 41 miles, with 19 miles on pavement. (Details about West Dry Canyon and Santa Barbara Canyon can be found in *Guide 5, Santa Barbara County*.)

Apache Canyon Road
Route/Trail: #8N06
Length: 9 mile one ways
Level of Difficulty: Easy
Elevation: 3300' - 4300'; 1000' diff.
Water: None
Parking: Turnouts along Highway 33, or Apache Canyon Road past ranch fields
Campgrounds: Nettle Spring
Nearest Services: Halfway Station Cafe; Ventucopa; New Cuyama

Apache Canyon Road heads east from Highway 33 at the bridge at milepost 53.83. It is graded and open to motor vehicles. Off-highway vehicles travel in the sandy wash most of the way, parallel to the road. The new Chumash Wilderness is located nearby on the south and west slopes of Mt. Pinos and Mt.

Abel, and the wilderness boundary parallels the upper 2.5 miles of Apache Canyon Road on the north side and runs around the north and east sides of Nettle Springs Camp at the end of the road. San Emigdio Mesa Trail #22W21 is now in the wilderness area and bicycles are prohibited there. Water is not available at Nettle Spring Camp, so bring your own supply.

Bear Canyon Trail
Route/Trail: #24W04
Length: 2.7 miles one way
Level of Difficulty: Very difficult in the gorge
Elevation: 4600' - 3650'; 950' diff.
Water: Seasonal water in Bear Canyon streams
Parking: Turnouts on Highway 33 near mile 47.47 or 46.2
Campgrounds: None
Nearest Services: Ozena Forest Service Station; Halfway Station Cafe

Ride this as a loop trip using the highway to get up to the upper trailhead at mile 45.27 on a sharp bend in the road. Park near the lower trail end at mile 47.47 and ride up the Highway the 2.2 miles first or park at wide turnout at about halfway on the north side of the road (46.2 miles) Ride up to the upper trailhead, down the trail, and back up one mile.

The upper and lower one-mile sections of this trail are rideable, but a 0.7-mile middle section passes through a narrow gorge and is very steep with several stream crossings. I recommend walking the entire gorge section.

Just off the highway at mile 45.27 a dirt road heads steeply down to the north about 100 feet. A locked gate on the west marks the trail. Here you descend into a tributary canyon and cross a series of small linked hillside meadows. At about the half-mile mark, where you are heading south, the trail switchbacks to the right and down the canyon (a lesser trail continues south). You descend and cross a small stream and farther along, after that stream joins another one, you cross the combined stream. Then you cross a dry stream and go up to the Deal Canyon Trail junction at 1.1 miles. (That trail enters the Dick Smith Wilderness just west of the junction.)

The next 0.7 mile down Bear Canyon is in a beautiful sandstone gorge with many oak and fir trees. However, the trail is very steep and slippery from leaves, so walking is recommended. The last mile is fairly straight and level to the highway.

—APPENDIX—

First Aid – *by Réanne Douglass*

Several years ago on a mountain biking trip, I miscalculated a sharp turn on a sandy stretch of dirt road, went flying and turned my right shin into raw meat. I didn't have a first aid kit with me. Why bother?After all, I was cycling off-road, no traffic around, and I planned to be gone just part of the day. When I got home, I took a shower, cleaned my wound and applied some antibiotic cream. Three days later, Don had to carry me to the doctor. A staph infection – that took three pain-filled weeks to control – had set in. *Don't be careless like I was.* Carry and use a First Aid Kit. You can purchase one at bike shops or sporting goods stores, or you can make your own. For day rides, we suggest the following items:

8 Bandaids 1" x 3"
6 Antiseptic Swabs or
   1 oz. Hydrogen Peroxide
1 Roll Adhesive Tape
1 Moleskin 3" x 4"
1 Single-Edge Razor Blade
Sunscreen 15 SPF or more

8 Aspirin Tablets or Aspirin Substitute
8 Gauze Pads 3" x 3"
4 Antacid Tablets
1 Elastic Bandage
1 Needle
Waterproof Matches (in film can)
Prescription Medicine (if applicable)

IMBA Rules of the Trail

1. **Ride on open trails only.** Respect trail and road closures (ask if not sure), avoid possible trespass on private land, obtain permits and authorization as may be required. Federal and State wilderness areas are closed to cycling.
2. **Leave no trace.** Be sensitive to the dirt beneath you. Even on open trails, you should not ride under conditions where you will leave evidence of your passing, such as on certain soils shortly after a rain. Observe the different types of soils and trail construction; practice low-impact cycling. This also means staying on the trail and not creating any new ones. Be sure to pack out at least as much as you pack in.
3. **Control your bicycle!** Inattention for even a second can cause disaster. Excessive speed maims and threatens people; there is no excuse for it!
4. **Always yield trail.** Make known your approach well in advance. A friendly greeting (or bell) is considerate and works well; startling someone may cause loss of trail access. Show your respect when passing others by slowing to a walk or even stopping. Anticipate that other trail users may be around corners or in blind spots.
5. **Never spook animals.** All animals are startled by an unannounced approach, a sudden movement, or a loud noise. This can be dangerous for you, others, and the animals. Give animals extra room and time to adjust to you. In passing, use special care and follow the directions of horseback riders (ask if uncertain). Running cattle and disturbing wild animals is a serious offense. Leave gates as you found them, or as marked.
6. **Plan ahead.** Know your equipment, your ability, and the area in which you are riding – and prepare accordingly. Be self-sufficient at all times, wear a helmet, keep your machine in good repair, and carry necessary supplies for changes in weather or other conditions. A well-executed trip is satisfying to you and not a burden or offense to others.

TOPO MAPS & GUIDEBOOKS FROM FINE EDGE PRODUCTIONS

MOUNTAIN BIKING AND RECREATION TOPO MAPS

Santa Monica Mountains, ISBN 0-938665-23-5	$9.95
Eastern High Sierra–Mammoth, June, Mono, ISBN 0-938665-21-9	$9.95
San Bernardino Mountains, ISBN 0-938665-32-4	$9.95
North Lake Tahoe Basin, ISBN 1-879866-06-4	$8.95
South Lake Tahoe Basin, ISBN 1-879866-07-2	$8.95

MOUNTAIN BIKING GUIDEBOOKS

Guide 1, Owens Valley and Inyo County, Second Edition, ISBN 0-938665-01-4	$9.95
Guide 2, Mammoth Lakes and Mono County, Third Edition, ISBN 0-938665-15-4	$9.95
Guide 3A, Lake Tahoe South, Third Edition, ISBN 0-938665-27-8	$10.95
Guide 3B, Lake Tahoe North, Second Edition, ISBN 0-938665-07-3	$9.95
Guide 4, Ventura County and the Sespe, Third Edition, ISBN 0-938665-18-9	$9.95
Guide 5, Santa Barbara County, Third Edition, ISBN 0-938665-04-9	$9.95
Guide 7, Santa Monica Mountains, Second Edition, ISBN 0-938665-10-3	$9.95
Guide 8, Saugus District, Angeles N.F. with Mt. Pinos, ISBN 0-938665-09-8	$9.95
Guide 9, San Gabriel Mountains, Angeles N.F., ISBN 0-938665-11-1	$9.95
Guide 10, San Bernardino Mountains, ISBN 0-938665-16-2	$10.95
Guide 11, Orange County and Cleveland National Forest, ISBN 0-938665-17-0	$9.95
Guide 12, Riverside County & Coachella Valley, ISBN 0-938665-24-3	$10.95
Guide 13, Reno/Carson City, ISBN 0-938665-22-7	$10.95

OTHER GUIDEBOOKS AND MAPS

Mountain Biking Northern California's Best 100 Trails, ISBN 0-938665-31-6	$14.95
Mountain Biking Southern California's Best 100 Trails, ISBN 0-938665-20-0	$14.95
Favorite Pedal Tours of Northern California, ISBN 0-938665-12-X	$12.95
What Shall We Do Tomorrow–Mammoth Lakes Sierra, ISBN 0-938665-30-8	$10.95
What Shall We Do Tomorrow–North Lake Tahoe/Truckee, ISBN 0-9633056-0-3	$8.95
What Shall We Do Tomorrow–South Tahoe/Carson Pass, ISBN 0-9633056-1-1	$10.95
Ski Touring the Eastern High Sierra, ISBN 0-938665-08-1	$8.95
Exploring California's Channel Islands, an Artist's View, ISBN 0-938665-00-6	$6.95
Cape Horn–One Man's Dream, One Woman's Nightmare, ISBN 0-938665-29-4	$19.95
Exploring Vancouver Island's West Coast–A Cruising Guide, ISBN 0-938665-20-0	$36.95
Adventurer's Guide to the Sierra Nevada–travel version, ISBN 0-9619827-3-X	$9.95
Adventurer's Guide to the Sierra Nevada–lam. wall mural, ISBN 0-9619827-4-8	$19.95

Additional books and maps in process; manuscripts are solicited.
For current titles and prices, please send SASE.
To order any of these items, see you local dealer or order direct. Please include $2.50 for shipping. California residents add sales tax. 20% discount on orders of 5 or more items.

Fine Edge Productions, Route 2, Box 303, Bishop, California 93514